LEO STRAUSS, PHILOSOPHER

European Vistas

EDITED BY
Antonio Lastra
and
Josep Monserrat-Molas

SUNY PRESS

Published by State University of New York Press, Albany

Printed in the United States of America

For information, contact State University of New York Press, Albany, NY
www.sunypress.edu

Production, Jenn Bennett
Marketing, Michael Campochiaro

Library of Congress Cataloging-in-Publication Data

Leo Strauss, philosopher : European vistas / edited by Antonio Lastra and Josep Monserrat-Molas.

pages cm. — (SUNY series in the thought and legacy of Leo Strauss)

Includes bibliographical references and index.

ISBN 978-1-4384-6133-5 (hc : alk. paper) — ISBN 978-1-4384-6134-2 (pb : alk. paper)
ISBN 978-1-4384-6135-9 (e-book) 1. Strauss, Leo. I. Lastra, Antonio, editor.

B945.S84L46 2016

181'.06—dc23

2015030794

10 9 8 7 6 5 4 3 2 1

In memoriam
George Anastaplo (1925–2014), Constitutionalist
Stanley Rosen (1929–2014), Metaphysician

CONTENTS

Preface and Acknowledgments ix

Abbreviations xxiii

Antonio Lastra
A Proem 1

Carlo Altini
Philosophy and History of Philosophy 15

Alessandra Fussi
Loyalty and Love of Wisdom in Plato's Republic 43

Jordi R. Sales-Coderch
Engaged Citizenship 67

Mauro Farnesi Camellone
The City and Stranger 81

Till Kinzel
Lessing's Importance for the Philosopher 101

Josep Monserrat-Molas
An Epilogue 117

Notes on Contributors 137

Index 141

PREFACE AND ACKNOWLEDGMENTS

> ἀγὼνγὰρ καὶ ὁ προαγὼν καὶ μυστήρια τὰ πρὸμυστηρίων,
> οὐδὲὀκνήσεισυγχρήσασθαι φιλοσοφίας καὶ τῆςἄλλης
> προπαιδείας τοῖς καλλίστοιςτὰ ὕπομνήματα ἡμιν.
>
> —Clement of Alexandria
> *Stromata*[1] I. i.15.1–4

The University of Freiburg's announcement of plans to transform the philosophy chair, which was held in the first half of the twentieth century by Edmund Husserl and Martin Heidegger—who gave his controversial inaugural address as rector there on *The Self-Assertion of the German University*—has stirred up the quiet and sometimes stagnant waters of the academic community both within and outside Germany with the force of a flood. The replacement of the prestigious chair by a junior professor's post in logic and analytic philosophy of language not only signals an erosion in the professional status of the post's occupant, but is also an evidence that the modern adage—"there are nowadays professors of philosophy, but not philosophers"—is, to some extent, right. The adage, though, does go on to say that "yet it is admirable to profess [philosophy] because it was once admirable to live." So were Husserl and Heidegger philosophers or professors of philosophy? In his inaugural address, Heidegger referred to "teachers and students" as "followers" of "leaders who at all times are themselves led" (*Die Gefolschaft der Lehrer und Schüler* [. . .] *zuvörderst und jederzeit die Führer selbst Geführte sind*). Whatever the rationale for or interpretations of Heidegger's address, it may at least be said that his address is based on a particular reading of Plato's *Republic*, and that one of the keys to that reading lies in the careful selection of the final quotation and in the deliberate omission of its context. We return to Plato shortly.[2]

The distinction between a philosopher and a professor of philosophy is an important one. In Heideggerian circles, "professor of philosophy" was used to disparage Ernst Cassirer, Germany's most distinguished professor of philosophy of the time, more distinguished than Heidegger who had just succeeded Husserl at Freiburg. The matter arose in the celebrated debate in Davos in 1929 on the philosophy of Kant (Was he a philosopher himself or a professor of philosophy?) and doubtless arose out of the ancient *diaphora* between Socrates and the Sophists established by Plato in the dialogues, on the threshold of the history of philosophy, and perhaps even out of a suspicion that the dialogues themselves did not contain the true teachings of Plato, somehow paradoxically reserved for at the Academy. Socrates's apology to the city of Athens was that he had never been anybody's teacher. Taking this last perspective, the professor of philosophy would be the authentic philosopher.[3]

Leo Strauss, a member in his youth of what has been called the "Marburg constellation," together with Karl Löwith, Hans-Georg Gadamer, Jacob Klein, Gerhard Krüger, and Hannah Arendt (among the philosophy students), and Max Kommerell and Erich Auerbach (among the philology students),[4] shared their common impression that they stood before a philosopher when they were in Heidegger's presence. Conversely, Strauss believed that Cassirer, who had been the supervisor of his thesis on Jacobi and the problem of knowledge while he had studied at the University of Hamburg, was merely a professor of philosophy.[5] Towards the end of his life, however, Strauss came to share both in public and in private that in comparison with Husserl's philosophy as a rigorous science, the "fantastic hopes" of Heidegger seem "more to be expected from visionaries than from philosophers." Strauss also shared that "after many years it has become clear to me what is really false in him: a great intelligence in a kitsch soul [*Mir ist jetzt nach langen Jahre klar geworden, was eigentlich an ihm falsch ist: ein phänomenaler Intellekt, der auf einer* Kitsch-*Seele ist*]."[6]

As ironic as the concept of a "sociology of philosophy" may sound today—and that is what Strauss would eventually call the problem of the relationship between philosophy and politics—charting the contours of this province of the sociology of knowledge compels one to inquire in earnest into the position of the philosopher. What place does he or she occupy in any society—within and outside the Academy, as a professor, and as a citizen—and what is his or her relationship with the powers that be, including the constitutionally elected and responsible authorities within contemporary democracies?

Perhaps it is not a matter of rhetorical excess to say that nowadays there are no philosophers, nor will there even be professors of philosophy in the future. Of course, the distinction between the life and the profession of the philosopher is not insurmountable. It does, however, highlight certain difficulties and requires a radical honesty. This is so because philosophy as a profession is public or political, and it has been losing its genuinely free and liberal status as society has claimed it as a program of study that has become obligatory or supererogatory for all citizens. A professor of philosophy is not necessarily a sophist, but society has always been the greatest of the sophists. If nothing of what we nowadays call "knowledge transfer" takes place, then philosophy is impracticable. At present, the teaching of philosophy has made all teachers or professors of philosophy into servants or functionaries of the society or state.

To ask what there may be of philosophy in the formal (i.e., social) teaching of philosophy is to come face-to-face with the consequences of an ancillary or propedeutic tradition with regard to medieval theology or modern science. Naturally, philosophy can be conceived of as privately taught and even as self-taught, but that would take us back, on the one hand, to a historical situation in which we would recognize none of the contents of a contemporary philosophy program and, on the other hand, to the *rêveries* of a solitary rambler. In every sense, the First Amendment to the United States Constitution, which safeguards freedom of expression, delimits our situation and elicits a paradox that is tough to resolve. Are the freedom of speech and *libertas philosophandi* comparable? Is a teacher or professor of philosophy, whose constitutional framework is based on the freedom of expression, free to philosophize? When he was still a young professor of philology at the University of Basel, Nietzsche wrote that the content of Plato's *Republic* went beyond anything that παρρησία could permit even in the freest state. The freest state that Plato or Nietzsche had *ad oculos* was infinitely less free than any free state at the present time. Does the freedom of expression of the freest state today permit the literal exposition of Plato's *Republic*?[7]

The term παρρησία appears twice in the *Republic*, once in reference to democracy and other to tyranny. According to Socrates, the inhabitants of a democracy will, above all, be free, and the city will be full of freedom and "frankness" (as the freedom of expression of the ancients is usually translated, 557b); and in the same way, some who have raised up the tyrant will dare to "speak frankly" (567b).[8] In the *Laws*, where the term appears more often than in any other work in the Platonic corpus, the Stranger praises the "freedom of speech" of the Persians, and although his proposals disconcert the old Spartan, the old Cretan grants him the "freedom of speech" needed to lay out all the laws (694a–b, 806c–d).[9] Could a professor of philosophy nowadays present the content of Plato's dialogues literally in his or her philosophy classes? Is it not the "citizenship," as Protagoras says, that is now the authority that holds the position once held by medieval theology or modern science and uses all the means at its disposal so that philosophy serves as preparation, ever available to train good citizens? In a passage of the *Republic* that is difficult to interpret (558a), Socrates suggests that the philosopher "stalks" among the πολιτείᾳ (which we could at least provisionally translate as "citizenship" or "regime of the city") "as a hero" (περινοστεῖ ὥσπερ ἥρως). This is an almost incomprehensible phrase that translators have conveyed as "like some spirit from another world" (James Adam) or "*comme des revenants*" (Émile Chambry); and it corresponds to the later comparison of the philosopher with the "lotus-eaters" (560c; cf. 621c; "lotus-eaters" would later be used to characterize the Epicureans, i.e., philosophers in general).[10]

Far from taking the step from myth to logos that the city seems to expect from philosophy, Socrates prefers myth to frankness or free speech (376d, 614b, 621b). The repetition of the verb καταβαίνω suggests precisely that the civilized life demands a return descent into the cave (328c–d, 359d–e, 511b–c, 516e–517a, 519c–d, 520c, 539e, 614d–e). (The verb καταβαίνω appears in the *Republic* as many times as it does in the rest of the Platonic corpus.) But going back down into the cave is possible only if one knows how to read the *Republic*. The relationship between philosophy and writing is inseparable from that between philosophy and reading: learning how to read is a prerequisite for the teaching of philosophy. Does the city expect a professor of philosophy to teach reading? What kind of book could a professor of philosophy write today? Does the freedom of expression allow the patience needed to read the Platonic dialogues in the way they were written? Nietzsche, a master of slow reading, knew perfectly well that the freest state can censor by means of freedom too.

In fact, philosophical writing is not based on *libertas philosophandi* but on logographic necessity (τινὰ ἀνάγκην λογογραφικὴν, *Phaedrus,* 264b). The philosophical writer does not exercise the freedom of expression to which he or she would be entitled, because the philosophical life obeys the laws of natural necessity. In the decisive respects, obedience to the laws of natural necessity entails what we, in modern times, understand as civil disobedience. The strict relationship between the civil disobedience of philosophy and the writing of the United States Constitution is one of the most important chapters in modern philosophy, but at the same time one of the least well-known. A comparison of the writing of the United States Constitution and the reticent writing of the ancients prompts the realization that both the ancient philosophers and the writers of the Constitution were founders of cities (οἰκισταὶ πόλεως, *Resp.* 379a). Something in the character of professors of philosophy who admire philosophy and aspire to live a civilized life compels us—with all grace of nature—to emulate their work of founding.[11]

Traditionally the imitation of philosophical writing—the emulation of the city of words—is the commentary. A commentator, Strauss cautions, could sometimes be much bolder than the author insofar as nobody expects to find the originality of a worldview in his or her commentary. But if, as Nietzsche suggests, the gods too philosophize, why should the commentators not do so as well? Despite what may seem an obvious fact in a period marked by the proliferation of opinions, we have lost the habit of commentary, which, at least in the decisive stages of education, is nearly irreplaceable. To competence in reading, the habit of commentary adds (or added) a sense of the profoundly human admiration that binds the reader to the author and the author's work. Like any habit, the habit of commentary takes time and flourishes in its own time. That is the reason why a good commentator combines moral virtues and dianoetic virtues. If only for the fact that he seeks learning through commentary, teaching to learn through reading (*lesende lernen*), the work of Strauss, perhaps the last of the major Western commentators, would warrant being read closely and with gratitude.

The "philosophy of the commentators," as Richard Sorabji calls it, is based on the intuition that the history of philosophy is itself philosophy, an intuition rarely shared by today's historians of philosophy: the commentators were as much philosophers as historians of philosophy, no mere antiquarians or unquestioning disciples of a school or teacher.[12] However, unlike Sorabji's categorization of the philosophy of the commentators—psychology (in which he includes ethics and religion), physics, logic, and metaphysics—a categorization influenced by the Aristotelian analytic tradition, Strauss found in the commentaries of the Jewish and Islamic philosophers of the Middles Ages an access key to Plato's philosophy construed as a political philosophy.

The Platonic political philosophy of Strauss is a first-order contribution to the philosophy of the commentators, to the history of philosophy, and to philosophy understood as σκέψις "in the original sense of the term, *i.e.*, [as] the actual quest for the truth which is animated by the conviction that that quest alone makes life worth living, and which is fortified by the distrust of man's natural propensity to rest satisfied with satisfying, if unevident or unproven, convictions."[13] The commentary of political philosophy understood as first philosophy, for Strauss, was part of a conception of philosophy that differed hugely from what Plato, in the *Republic*, called "love of the city" (φιλόπολις). "Without cities, no philosophers," but the philosopher does not find his or her homeland in the city.[14] Philosophy, political philosophy, σκέψις, first philosophy—these form a set of philosophemes that contradict the inherited epistemology of the Theory of Forms and the immortality of the soul, about which Alfarabi remained scrupulously silent.

The "change of orientation" that led Strauss to a close reading of the way in which heterodox thinkers had written their books would not have been possible if he had not overcome the "powerful prejudice": that a return to premodern philosophy is impossible. The premodern philosophy to which Strauss would return time and again until the end of his life was Plato's political philosophy; and the manner in which heterodox thinkers had written their books was to require the discovery or rediscovery—to the extent that Strauss saw Alfarabi, Maimonides, Lessing, and Nietzsche as his predecessors—of a forgotten kind of writing: esoteric or reticent writing, "writing between the lines." Strauss was convinced that his investigations would "force historians sooner or later to abandon the complacency with which they claim to know what certain great thinkers thought, to admit that the thought of the past is much more enigmatic than it is generally held to be, and to begin to wonder whether the historical truth is not as difficult of access as the philosophical truth."[15] That Strauss's own writing followed the prescripts of esoteric, reticent or between-the-lines writing, and that these lines were delicately and yet firmly drawn by logographic necessity, are some of the most widespread appreciations (or accusations) voiced by the supporters (or detractors) of his work. Close examination of Strauss's writing in English in light of what he had written in German up until the time of his change of orientation—that is, when he ceased being a student of philosophy to become a professor of philosophy, officially or socially as a professor of political science—enables us to see his work, taken as a whole, as a commentary in the original sense of the term. Strauss's first study of classical antiquity included in its title the phrase "the taste of Xenophon" (i.e., philosophy), a taste that went beyond ancient poetics or Enlightenment esthetics.

In the margins of Strauss's reticent writing, Arthur M. Melzer has written a scrupulously academic book *Philosophy Between the Lines* and the lost history of esoteric writing.[16] Paradoxically Melzer's conventional or exoteric presentation strengthens the conviction that esoteric writing is neither an invention of Strauss nor a poetic or esthetic feature of style that can be pushed to one side with impunity when understanding philosophers. An esoteric book is an imitation of nature: if the cave of opinion hides reality and if philosophy is to replace opinions with the knowledge of reality, then esotericism becomes a technique of interpretation superior to most of the techniques used in contemporary hermeneutics. The "rhetoric of concealment would be most useful, perhaps even necessary, to disclose reality as it is in hiddenness." In the most deliberately Straussian pages of the book, Melzer poses "the problem of the philosopher," a problem argued to be closer to the nature of things than, for example, "the Jewish problem" or the "race question," (or the "gender question"):

> It would require a wonderfully learned and subtle work of history to describe all the myriad forms that changing times and circumstances have given to the relations between philosophers and the religio-political communities in which they have lived. Such a work [. . .] has never been undertaken. Yet such analysis is essential if we are to gain an authentic understanding of the history of Western philosophy.

An authentic understanding of the history of philosophy calls for commentary—that is, attentive to both the reticence and the literal sense of the writing of philosophers.

But a world lacking the most basic patience is doomed to lose the ability to read. The issue of reading, of interpretation, is also a fundamental issue of contemporary society, though it is not necessarily so for the societies of the past or the societies of the future. The issue had already begun to dwindle in importance in Strauss's time. What, if not this, was the "fundamental question" that did not deserve to suffer the fate that Strauss expected of Jonathan Wild's book on Plato?[17] The fundamental issue was not the mere technical question of an alternative modern hermeneutics to the prevailing historicism of the time, but the issue of a philosophical education (cf. *Resp.* 376e) to give effect to the political thought of the classics; that is, to understand the extent to which the relationship between philosophy and the city is a matter in dispute. Strauss had learned from the Jewish and Islamic commentaries that the philosophical life is self-sufficient (from Aristotle to Nietzsche, a hermit's life), but that it had to be lived beyond the boundaries of the city so as not to put the life of the philosopher in jeopardy. But how should one orient oneself so that the never-completed task of reconciling the homogeneity of nature's laws and the heterogeneity of human purposes, without resorting to reductionism, is a sustainable one? How can one sustain oneself between the free recognition of nature's necessity and the recognition demanded by the laws of the city? One attempt to transmit the *sképsis* or *zêtêsis* of philosophy has been through texts, acknowledging the limitations—the logographic necessity—of writing. Strauss applied himself to an art of writing that enacted noetic activity as the ability to read. Through the study of commentaries, he was to discover a way around the text's authority while at the same time acknowledging that a text constituted an authority. The commentary, though it is an autopsy, can breathe life back into a text; it breaks the text down to reassemble it. But only if one knows how to read and only if the art of reading corresponds to the art of writing. Giving authority to a text clears ground for investigation. How much freedom is or is not gained by the practice of commentary after a disciplined preparation? Disciplined preparation readies the reader to regard the work not as doctrine or dogma, which would call for joining in or adherence, but as a practice that above all seeks to protect the practice of philosophy itself. Strauss found one of these protections, a paradoxical and oblique way of communicating that he wished to share.

The authors of these chapters are European professors of philosophy. "European Vistas," the subtitle of the volume, is an echo of Walt Whitman's *Democratic Vistas.* We would like to remember that Europe lacks a constitutional writing that is comparable to the United States Constitution. The lack of a constitutional writing is concomitant with the lack of a free philosophical writing. As a consequence, each of the chapters of this volume and the order in which the chapters appear, follow scrupulously the merciless laws of logographic necessity. Each chapter is strictly a commentary on Strauss's work, and each author is, therefore, a commentator on a work that—as Strauss wrote of the work of Hermann Cohen, Heidegger's predecessor at Marburg—is in itself "a commentary on an already highly technical text and hence like a man whose thought is derivative and traditional in the extreme; and yet he surprises time and again with strikingly original and weighty thoughts."[18]

Our special thanks must go to Professor Kenneth Hart Green for his invitation to put this book together. We are indebted to him both for his superlative professional skills and for his sense of humanity. We would also like to extend our gratitude to Doctor Michael Rinella and his editorial team at SUNY Press and to the two anonymous readers of the work for their suggestions, which we have very much taken into account. Over time, we have learned from the teachings of Martin David Yaffe, Heinrich Meier, Chris Cholmo, Rémi Brague, and Philippe Bénéton. The study is unending. Our thanks go to all.

A version of the first chapter, "A Proem," appeared in Spanish as a preliminary study of the translation of a series of texts by Leo Strauss. It was published under the title of *Sin ciudades no hay filósofos* (translated by Antonio Lastra and Raúl Miranda, and published by Tecnos, Madrid, 2014). This chapter is a part of the research project "Hacia una Historia Conceptual comprehensiva: giros filosóficos y culturales" (FFI2011–24473) from the Economy and Competitiveness Office of the Spanish Government. For this preface, we have also used some excerpts from notes on Leo Strauss published in the journal *Ápeiron: Estudios de filosofía* (Madrid, 2014). In both cases, we would like to thank the publishers for their kind permission. The doctoral student Víctor Páramo Valero has produced the index of names. And lastly we would like to thank Joel Graham and Carlos Valero Serra for their help in the translations into English. At all times, the translation has followed the Straussian rule of thumb to proceed *in ultimitate literalitatis.*

ANTONIO LASTRA AND JOSEP MONSERRAT-MOLAS
l'Eliana (Valencia) and El Prat de Llobregat (Barcelona),
March 2015

NOTES

1. "For there is a contest, and the prelude to the contest; and there are some mysteries before other mysteries, [and so] our book will not shrink from making use of what is best in philosophy and other preparatory instruction" (*The Ante-Nicene Fathers*, vol. 2,

trans. Arthur Cleveland Coxe, [1885], slightly modified). See Leo Strauss, "Exoteric Teaching," ed. Hannes Kerber, in *Reorientation: Leo Strauss in the 1930s*, eds. Martin D. Yaffe and Richard S. Ruderman (New York: Palgrave Macmillan, 2013), 275–292, 279nxviii.

2. Martin Heidegger, *Die Selbstbehauptung der deutschen Universität. Das Rektorat 1933/342*, (Frankfurt am Main: Vittorio Klostermann, 1990). The efficient cause of the decision of the University of Freiburg of transforming the chair was the publication of Heidegger's *Schwarze Hefte* (*Black Notebooks*), which reignited the controversy about the relationship of his thought to politics as well as his anti-Semitism. See also Richard Wolin, "National Socialism, World Jewry, and the History of Being: Heidegger's Black Notebooks," in *Jewish Review of Books* (Summer, 2014); Peter E. Gordon, "Heidegger in Black," in *The New York Review of Books* (October, 2014), and Jürgen Kaube, "Martin? Edmund!" in *Frankfurter Allgemeine Zeitung* (27 February 2015). See also Yvonne Sherratt, *Hitler's Philosophers* (New Haven: Yale University Press, 2013), and Peter Trawny, *Heidegger und der Mythos der jüdischen Weltverschwörung* (Frankfurt am Main: Vittorio Klostermann, 2015). (Leo Strauss is the first philosopher quoted by Trawny.)
3. See *Apol.* 33a (ἐγὼ δὲ διδάσκαλος μὲν οὐδενὸς πώποτ᾽ἐγενόμην) and *Prot.* 319a. Socrates is ironic with Protagoras's "promise" (τὸ ἐπάγγελμα ὃ ἐπαγγέλλομαι) to make people good citizens and speaks of the civic science (ἆρα, ἔφην ἐγώ, ἕπομαί σου τῷ λόγῳ; δοκεῖς γάρ μοι λέγειν τὴν πολιτικὴν τέχνην καὶ ὑπισχνεῖσθαι ποιεῖν ἄνδρας ἀγαθοὺς πολίτας; the Heideggerian equivalent for "citizen" is *volk* or *unsselbst*). The correspondent verb to ἐπάγγελμα is ἐπάγγέλλεσθαι, and in Latin is *profiteri*, from which came the technical term *professor*, with which the Sophists would be appointed during the Roman Empire. See Philostratus, *Vita Sophistorum*, Praef.
4. Matthias Bormuth and Ulrich von Bülow, eds., *Marburger Hermeneutik zwischen Tradition und Krise* (Göttingen:Wallstein-Verlag, 2008). The "Marburg constellation" gets its strength from the rejection of the Marburg School, of which Cassirer was the last representative. One thing that has to be taken into account in order

to understand Strauss's Platonic political philosophy is the neo-Kantian interpretation of Plato.

5. On the only occasion that Strauss wrote about Cassirer concerning the posthumous *The Myth of the State* (1946), Strauss described Cassirer's teaching as "aestheticist." *What Is Political Philosophy? And Other Studies* [1959] (Chicago: University of Chicago Press,1988), 292–296. See the innovative studies of Rodrigo Chacón, "On a Forgotten Kind of Grounding: Strauss, Jacobi, and the Phenomenological Critique of Modern Rationalism," in the *Review of Politics* 76 (2014): 589–617; and "Strauss and Husserl," in *Idealistic Studies* 23 (forthcoming).
6. See "Philosophy as Rigorous Science and Political Philosophy" (1971), in *Studies in Platonic Political Philosophy* (Chicago: University of Chicago Press, 1985), 29–37; and the letter to Gershom Scholem of 17 July 1973. The letter appeared in *Gesammelte Schriften*, Band 3: *Hobbes' politische Wissenschaft, und zugehörige Schriften—Briefe*2 (2001), eds. Heinrich Meier and Wiebke Meier (Stuttgart: J.B. Metzler Verlag, 2008), 770. In the same letter, Strauss wrote to Scholem that his shared the sentiments of Averroes's motto: *moriatur anima mea mortem philosophorum*. See also Stanley Rosen, "Contributions to 'Contributions': Remarks on Heidegger's *Beiträge*," in *Essays in Philosophy. Ancient and Modern*, ed. Martin Black (South Bend, IN: St. Augustine's Press, 2013), 2:153–163.
7. In a remarkable book, David Roochnik wonders "whether the only honest response to the *Republic* would be a comprehensive, line-by-line commentary": (*Beautiful City: The Dialectical Character of Plato's Republic* (Ithaca, NY: Cornell University Press, 2003), 1. That kind of commentary, typical of the Jewish and Islamic philosophy of the Middle Ages, is almost entirely lacking in Western literature. Roochnik suggests that such an "impatient time" as ours precludes such exegesis, whose premise would be the "extraordinary level of internal coherence" of the *Republic*.
8. Allan Bloom translates παρρησία as "free speech"; in the second, he translates παρρησιάζεσθαι as "speak frankly." See *The Republic of Plato*, ed. Allan Bloom (New York: Basic Books, 1991), 235, 246.

9. See *The Laws of Plato*, trans. Thomas L. Pangle (Chicago: University of Chicago Press, 1988), 78, 196.
10. Schleiermacher's translation deserves to be reproduced: "Ist die Humanität gegen manche der nach dem Gesetze Verurteilten nicht etwas Hübsches? Oder hast du in einem solchen Staate noch keine Leute nach ihrer Verurteilung zum Tode oder zur Verbannung nichtsdestoweniger dableiben und mitten in der Stadt auf und ab spazieren sehen? Als habe kein Mensch acht noch Auge auf ihn, stolziert ein solcher Kerl wie ein Held einher!" See Hannes Kerber, "Strauss and Schleiermacher on How to Read Plato: An Introduction to 'Exoteric Teaching,'" in *Reorientation*, 203–214.
11. See the work on constitutional writing of Leo Strauss's pupil George Anastaplo.
12. See Richard Sorabji, *ed.,The Philosophy of the Commentators 200–600 AD: A Sourcebook*, 3 vols. Vol. 1, *Psychology (with Ethics and Religion)*; vol. 2, *Physics*; vol. 3, *Logic and Metaphysics*. (Ithaca, NY: Cornell University Press, 2005).
13. Leo Strauss, "Farabi's *Plato*," in *Louis Ginzberg Jubilee Volume* (New York: American Academy for Jewish Research, 1945), 393. Alfarabi was known during the Middle Ages as the "second teacher." See Michael P. Zuckert and Catherine H. Zuckert, *Leo Strauss and the Problem of Political Philosophy* (Chicago: University of Chicago Press, 2014), chap. 6, "Why Strauss Is Not an Aristotelian."
14. See Leo Strauss and Jacob Klein, "A Giving of Accounts," in *Jewish Philosophy and the Crisis of Modernity. Essays and Lectures in Modern Jewish Thought*, ed. Kenneth Hart Green, (Albany: State University of New York Press, 1997), 465. Cf. *Resp.* 503a and 590e–592b, with Martin Heidegger, *Einführung in die Metaphysik* (1935), *Gesamtausgabe*, Band 40 (Frankfurt am Main: Vittorio Klostermann, 1983), 161–162 (116–117 of the 1953 second edition).
15. Leo Strauss, "On a Forgotten Kind of Writing," in *What Is Political Philosophy?* 232.
16. Arthur M. Melzer, *Philosophy Between the Lines. The Lost History of Esoteric Writing* (Chicago: University of Chicago Press, 2014), 139 ss., 144, 232–234. Melzer has compiled an authentic history of

esoteric writing in an online appendix: http://www.press.uchicago.edu/sites/melzer/.

17. See Leo Strauss, "On a New Interpretation of Plato's Political Philosophy," in *Social Research*, 13/3 (1946), 326–327. Significantly Strauss did not include this writing at any later collection.
18. Leo Strauss, "Preface to the English Translation," in *Spinoza's Critique of Religion* (1965), trans. E.M. Sinclair (Chicago: University of Chicago Press, 1997), 25. See the final chapter of *Studies in Platonic Political Philosophy* devoted to Cohen; the book begins with a chapter devoted to Husserl who was Heidegger's predecessor as professor of philosophy.

ABBREVIATIONS

AAPL: *The Argument and the Action of Plato's Laws* (1975). Chicago: University of Chicago Press, 1998.

CCWM: "Correspondence Concerning *Wahrheit und Methode*." In *The Independent Journal of Philosophy / Unabhängige Zeitschrift für Philosophie* 2:5 (1978): 5–12.

CM: *The City and Man* (1964). Chicago: University of Chicago Press, 1978.

ET: "Exoteric Teaching." Edited by Hannes Kerber. In *Reorientation: Leo Strauss in the 1930s*, edited by Martin D. Yaffe and Richard S. Ruderman, 275–292. New York: Palgrave Macmillan, 2013.

EW: *The Early Writings (1921–1932)*. Edited by Michael Zank. Albany: State University of New York Press, 2002.

FP: "Farabi's Plato." In *Louis Ginzberg Jubilee Volume*, edited by S.W. Baron, 357–393. New York: American Academy for Jewish Research, 1945. (reprinted with variations as "Introduction" to *Persecution and the Art of Writing* [1952], 22–37. Chicago: University of Chicago Press, 1988).

GS 1: *Gesammelte Schriften*, Band 1: *Die Religionskritik Spinozas und gehörige Schriften* (1996). Edited by Heinrich Meier. Stuttgart and Weimar: J. B. Metzler Verlag, 2008.

GS 2: *Gesammelte Schriften*, Band 2: *Philosophie und Gesetz—Frühe Schriften* (1998). Edited by Heinrich Meier and Wiebke Meier. Stuttgart and Weimar: J. B. Metzler Verlag, 2004.

GS 3: *Gesammelte Schriften*, Band 3: *Hobbes' politische Wissenschaft, und zugehörige Schriften—Briefe* (2001). Edited by Heinrich Meier, Wiebke Meier, and J.B. Metzler. Stuttgart: Verlag, 2008.

HFRPL: "How Fārābī read Plato's Laws." In *What Is Political Philosophy? And Other Studies* (1959), 134–154. Chicago: University of Chicago Press, 1988.

HPP: *History of Political Philosophy*. Edited by Leo Strauss and Joseph Cropsey. Chicago: University of Chicago Press, 1987.

JPCM: *Jewish Philosophy and the Crisis of Modernity. Essays and Lectures in Modern Jewish Thought*. Edited by Kenneth Hart Green. Albany: State University of New York Press, 1997.

LAM: *Liberalism Ancient and Modern* (1968). Chicago: University of Chicago Press, 1995.

LIGPP: "The Living Issues of German Postwar Philosophy," (1940). In *Leo Strauss and the Theologico-Political Problem*, edited by Heinrich Meier, 115–138. Cambridge: Cambridge University Press, 2006.

LNPAW: "Lecture Notes for *Persecution and the Art of Writing*" (1939). In *Reorientation: Leo Strauss in the 1930s*, edited by Martin D. Yaffe and R.S. Ruderman, 293–304. New York: Palgrave Macmillan, 2013.

LSMC: *Leo Strauss on Maimonides. The Complete Writings*. Edited by Kenneth Hart Green. Chicago: University of Chicago Press, 2013.

LSMM: *Leo Strauss on Moses Mendelssohn*. Edited by Martin D. Yaffe. Chicago: University of Chicago Press, 2012.

NIPPP: "On a New Interpretation of Plato's Political Philosophy." In *Social Research* 13, 1/4 (1946): 326–336.

NPR: "Notes on Philosophy and Revelation." In *Leo Strauss and the Theologico-Political Problem*, edited by Heinrich Meier, 172–279. New York: Cambridge University Press, 2006.

NRH: *Natural Right and History* (1953). Chicago: University of Chicago Press, 1965.

OCPH: "On Collingwood's Philosophy of History." In *Review of Metaphysics* 5 (1952): 559–586.

OPS: *On Plato's Symposium*. Edited by Seth Benardete. Chicago: University of Chicago Press, 2001.

OT: *On Tyranny. Including the Strauss-Kojève Correspondence*. Edited by Victor Gourevitch and Michael S. Roth. Chicago: University of Chicago Press, 2000.

PAW: *Persecution and the Art of Writing* (1952). Chicago: University of Chicago Press, 1988.

PL: *Philosophy and Law. Contributions to the Understanding of Maimonides and His Predecessors*. Translated by Eve Adler. Albany: State University of New York Press, 1995.

PR: "Progress or Return? The Contemporary Crisis in Western Civilization." In *Modern Judaism* 1, no. 1 (May, 1981): 17–45. The essay is reprinted in *The Rebirth of Classical Political Rationalism. An Introduction to the Thought of Leo Strauss*, edited by Thomas L. Pangle, 227–276. Chicago: University of Chicago Press, 1989.

PS: "The Problem of Socrates: Five Lectures." In *The Rebirth of Classical Political Rationalism. An Introduction to the Thought of Leo Strauss*, edited by Thomas L. Pangle, 103–183. Chicago: University of Chicago Press, 1989.

RCPP: *The Rebirth of Classical Political Rationalism. An Introduction to the Thought of Leo Strauss*. Edited by Thomas L. Pangle. Chicago: University of Chicago Press, 1989.

RKS: *Die Religionskritik Spinozas als Grundlage seiner Bibelwissenschaft. Untersuchungen zu Spinozas Theologisch-politischem Traktat*. Berlin: Akademia,1930. Reprinted in *GS 1*.

R: "Relativism." In *Relativism and the Study of Man*, edited by H. Schoeck and J.W. Wiggins, 135–157. Princeton: Van Nostrand, 1961, reprinted in *RCPP*, 13–26.

RR: "Reason and Revelation." In Heinrich Meier, *Leo Strauss and the Theologico-Political Problem*, translated by Marcus Brainard, 141–180. Cambridge: Cambridge University Press, 2006.

SA: *Socrates and Aristophanes* (1966). Chicago: University of Chicago Press, 1996.

SCR: *Spinoza's Critique of Religion*. Translated by Elsa M. Sinclair. Chicago: University of Chicago Press, 1997.

SPPP: *Studies in Platonic Political Philosophy* (1983). Chicago: University of Chicago Press, 1985.

SSTX: "The Spirit of Sparta or the Taste of Xenophon." In *Social Research*, 6/4 (1939): 502–536.

TM: *Thoughts on Machiavelli* (1958). Chicago: University of Chicago Press, 1995.
WIPP: *What Is Political Philosophy? And Other Studies* (1959). Chicago: University of Chicago Press, 1988.
XS: *Xenophon's Socrates.* Ithaca, NY: Cornell University Press, 1972.

A Proem

Antonio Lastra

ἐπεὶ καὶ τὸ λοιπὸν οὐ πάντων ῥᾷστον διελθεῖν.
τὸ ποῖον;
τίνα τρόπον μεταχειριζομένη πόλις φιλοσοφίαν οὐ διολεῖται.

—Plato
Resp. 497d

Every philosophy conceals a philosophy. The "philosophy of the future"—of which Friedrich Nietzsche's *Beyond Good and Evil* was only the prelude—could conceal, at least partially or between the lines, the philosophy of Leo Strauss (Kirchhain, Germany, 1899; Annapolis, United States, 1973).[1] The suggestion that the philosophy of Leo Strauss—forty years after his death, once the controversy about his political influence is over and when the world of readers has access to practically everything he wrote, and not only what he published—might be in itself a philosophy of the future, as paradoxical as it may seem applied to a thinker for whom reading the ancient writers and the biblical *teshuva* became the main lines of his considerations, would be based as much on the premise that philosophy as such has no tradition as on the difficulties involved in tracing its own history. The awkwardness of the philosopher in relation to historical sense is well-known.[2] Tradition and history always refer to a past—and a continuation of that past—that has overcome oblivion and has arrived, more or less altered, in the present. History and tradition refer to societies with their customs, opinions, and laws that, as peculiar and different as they might be, remain customs, opinions, and laws of society, of the same society, whatever its regime, which would not exist and would not be intelligible without a history and tradition. On the other hand, philosophy is a *regimen solitarii* or transpolitical. The philosopher would therefore be closer to a hermit concerned about the salvation of his soul *sub quaedam specie aeternitatis*, or about living according to Nature, than to a citizen concerned about the salvation or the government of his country. Only by transcending these customs, opinions, and laws, or in a situation of extreme necessity could he become guardian of the city or guardian of his brother. Even in this case, it would be very difficult to separate what is due to chance from what might be expected of the miraculous intervention of a particular providence or from dispensations of fate.[3] Society is necessarily conventional and religious, while philosophy is necessarily exceptional and unscrupulous: the philosopher's soul, unlike the body, is elsewhere. According to Nietzsche, in the writings of a hermit (*Einsiedler*), we perceive solitude and silence. The hermit is the guardian of the cave, which can be a labyrinth or a gold mine. The hermit's cave is his book: a hermit's book conceals a treasure. "The hermit—supposing that a philosopher always started as a hermit—never believes that the philosopher has expressed in his books his authentic and final opinions: aren't books written precisely to hide what we conceal inside us?"

In his only text specifically dedicated to Nietzsche—to a single book by Nietzsche—published shortly after his death, Strauss acknowledged that *Beyond Good and Evil* always "seemed" to him "the most beautiful of Nietzsche's books" and pointed out that, somehow, it was also "the only book published" by the author. The beauty of the book would be inseparable from its public nature.[4] Nietzsche would admit in *Ecce Homo* that *Beyond Good and Evil* was essentially a "critique of modernity." The philosophy of the future was beautifully presented in public as a critique of modernity; the critique of modernity should have resulted in modern society becoming a chapter of the past. The fact that modern society became a chapter of the past would be just a sign of the intrinsic brevity of tradition and history: world history, as the young Nietzsche had guessed, was, after all, just a minute. The publication and the beauty of a book of philosophy could be used, then, to hide "an even deeper cave": only the descent to that deeper cave, to the deepest cave, would allow the subsequent ascent to the closest cave to the surface and sunlight, to the "pure spirit and good in itself"; that is, the natural or Platonic cave. (In one of his sentences closest to the enigmatic and mysterious nature of Nietzsche's aphorisms, Strauss wrote that "the problem inherent in the surface of things, and only in the surface of things, is the heart of things.") Strauss said in relation to the form—the publication and beauty—of *Beyond Good and Evil* that Nietzsche would have platonized much more than what his "fight against Plato" might suggest: the fight against Plato, against the pure spirit and good in itself, would actually be the adequate preparation for the critique of modernity. The critique of modernity and the fight against Plato would have created, in any case, "a magnificent tension of the spirit," a tension that only the philosopher would be able to withstand.[5] However, without cities, there are no philosophers. Unlike the existence of society, the possibility of philosophy can never be taken for granted. The mere preservation of a philosophy does not guarantee its being practiced or transmitted: philosophy requires much more than mere preservation. Every philosophy conceals a philosophy to carefully preserve it but also to allow the Socratic question of how a city that does not want to perish should practice philosophy to be formulated.[6]

The tension of the spirit created by the fight against Plato and the critique of modernity is especially manifest when trying to translate the language of philosophy into the language of society. The relationship between philosophy and society is the central subject in Strauss's Platonic political philosophy and includes the question about philosophy itself: answering the question about what philosophy is requires elucidating the relationship between philosophy and society. Political philosophy is a response to the question about philosophy itself. Philosophy can destroy the society that falsely accuses it of being the cause of its destruction. Unable to perceive the pure spirit and the good in itself, the city accepts secondhand interpretations or opinions. The philosopher, by contrast, wants to find the original text (God or the world), wants to know everything, to know the articulations or the noetic heterogeneity of the whole.

From this perspective, we could read aphorism 28 in *Beyond Good and Evil* as if Strauss were the "transfiguring and ministerial" spirit (*verklärenden, complementären Geist*) that every text needs for its commentary.[7] The decisive position of aphorism 28, whose beginning refers to "the most difficult thing to render from one language into another," is given by the headings of aphorisms 27 ("It is difficult to be understood") and 29 ("It is the business of the very few to be independent"): untranslatability belongs, then, to the same pragmatic sphere as misunderstanding and independence. The difficulty of understanding the free spirits, the nuances of freethinking, the subtlety of interpretation, the privilege and the need for independence would be as characteristic of the philosophy of the future as of Strauss's philosophy. At the very heart of his argumentation, when he says that Lessing, unlike Goethe, was an "exception" in Germany, Nietzsche could not be referring only to his having been able, thanks to his "comedic nature," to translate Bayle or "flee" with Diderot and Voltaire, thus overcoming the inability of the German language to translate Petronius or Aristophanes—even if his prose could not have ultimately "imitated" Machiavelli. Nietzsche could not of course ignore that the anti-machiavellism of the German language was one of the clearest signs of the hypocrisy and philistinism of modern society—nor that, revealing "Plato's secret" (that is, that Plato never did truly reject Aristophanes), he was giving the keys to the old discord between philosophy and poetry (*Resp.* 607b). The imitation of Machiavelli and the discord between philosophy and poetry, exemplified by Thrasymachus's or Aristophanes's position in Plato's dialogues and by their relationship with Socrates, would be important topics of Strauss's philosophy.[8] But Nietzsche's identification of Lessing's freethinking and "the flight from Germany" (*die Flucht aus Deutschland*) in Lessing was crucial to understand how and why this philosophy would conceal itself in another or conceal itself a philosophy. Lessing's exception proved the rule of philosophy. Every philosophy, indeed, conceals more than one philosophy: Strauss concealed Lessing's philosophy in his own to turn his exception into the rule that he would follow in his way of reading and writing philosophy books.

The plan of *Beyond Good and Evil* required the second section on "Free Spirit" to be preceded by a section on "the prejudices of philosophers." The spirit would be free because it got rid of the philosophers' prejudices. The philosophers of the future, the "new philosophers" would be free spirits once "an old and stupid prejudice" had vanished and gone away. But Nietzsche distinguished his *Freie Geist* from *libre-penseurs, liberi pensatori, Freidenker* "or whatever all those brave defenders of modern ideas like to be called."[9] Lessing, meanwhile, had liked to call himself *Freigeist* almost from the beginning of his career as a writer and, as he wrote to his friend Moses Mendelssohn when that career was advanced enough to realize of the variety of his responsibilities towards the readers (as a playwright, poet, critic, scholar, theologian or philosopher), he was afraid that "by throwing away certain prejudices" he had "thrown away a little too much that I shall have to fetch back."[10] Strauss could find in Lessing both the free spirit and the investigator—or "antiquarian" (*Antiquar*) in Lessing's own word, whose meaning Strauss inverted in translating it from German into English—that was not afraid that his task consisted of recovering something, restoring a reading, which he had discarded before. The spirit could also (or perhaps only) be free by recovering some prejudices. The philosopher can hold prejudices or be forced to use them as a matter of prudence in his relationship with society. Lessing's imaginary flight from Germany would converge with Strauss's "[real] parting from Germany."

The reasons why Strauss concealed Lessing's philosophy may have had to do with his own escape from Germany and with the philosophy he would have to deal with in the United States as a "good European" ("we good Europeans and free spirits," in Nietzsche's words), educated in German universities in the interwar period, for whom the presence of Martin Heidegger in the classrooms had been an intellectual shock and whose Jewish background had not prevented him from discussing radically—thanks to his knowledge of the critique of religion in Spinoza and Hobbes's political philosophy—Carl Schmitt's concept of the political just before the arrival of Nazism. Setting himself apart from an Orthodox family education, Strauss felt the same Jewishness was sufficiently ambiguous to allow him initially to believe that Zionism was a viable solution to the Jewish problem and also, associating the prestige of German science with traditional Jewish exegesis, to study and edit the works of Mendelssohn, whom Strauss considered the founder of modern Judaism. In the United States, Strauss could answer the question about "why we remain Jews." Strauss would admit at the end of his life that in all these cases "Lessing was always at my elbow."[11]

If Lessing—not the Lessing of a certain tradition, but the true and unknown Lessing—had always been at his elbow, that could mean only one thing: that Strauss had always been on the side of philosophy. The fact that Strauss had always been on the side of philosophy excluded his being on the side of theology or politics, of political theology; that is, on the side of society. In the famous autobiographical preface to the English translation of his book on Spinoza, Strauss presented the "author" (the *ego ipsissimus*) as "a young Jew born and raised in Germany who found himself in the grips of the theologico-political predicament," and, in his only mention of Lessing, summed up in a single line all the works that young Jew had written in Europe: "Jacobi made public the fact that in Lessing's view there was no philosophy but the philosophy of Spinoza." Having always had Lessing at his elbow could mean that Strauss had always been on the side of Baruch Spinoza's philosophy, which did not exclude his having been on the side of a liberal and democratic society like the one Spinoza seemed to have defended, but would exclude his being on the side of a non-liberal or orthodox society. If revelation was the foundation of orthodoxy, Judaism could never be assimilated to a liberal society. The foundation of liberal society would be *libertas philosophandi*, which was the limit of modern Judaism interpretations, as any reader of Mendelssohn's *Jerusalem* could confirm. But neither could do Christianity, and that was the limit of the interpretations of Spinoza and Lessing.

In the last letter Lessing wrote to Mendelssohn, he expressed his craving to escape to "a country in Europe where there were neither Christians nor Jews." Since Islam is unthinkable without Jews or Christians, Lessing could refer to a modern secular society—like the society that could be established, for example, after the First Amendment to the Constitution of the United States—or to the ancient city. If, as Lessing knew perfectly well, the best of all possible constitutions would remain imperfect and the ancient city had its gods too, then that country in

Europe where to flee to could only be found in the old books of ancient writers: in the city of words, but not in the actual city.

In the last paragraph of the autobiographical preface, Strauss brought together, without mentioning them, Nietzsche and Lessing: the "change of orientation" that occurred in Strauss before taking flight or leave from Germany would have been to cast aside the powerful prejudice of thinking that a return to premodern philosophy was impossible. The return to premodern philosophy meant that there was another philosophy apart from Spinoza's or that the philosophy of Spinoza was essentially the same as premodern philosophy. It is possible, indeed, that all philosophers form a class of their own and that what unites all genuine philosophers is more important than what unites any philosopher with any group of nonphilosophers. Strauss shed light on this dilemma by paying attention to how heterodox thinkers of earlier times had written their books. Heterodox thinkers of earlier times were not able to take revelation literally. As a result, Strauss would read the *Theologico-Political Treatise* in a different way from the way he had read it when he was a young Jew who found himself in the grips of the theologico-political predicament and "understood Spinoza too literally because" he "did not read him literally enough."[12]

Literal reading discovers reticent writing. Literality and reticence are guidelines for the interpretation of Platonic political philosophy texts. The line "Jacobi made public the fact that in Lessing's view there was no philosophy but the philosophy of Spinoza" was as literal as it was reticent. Judging only by the mentions of Mendelssohn and Lessing found in books, articles and reviews published by Strauss in the United States since 1939—when his first study on Xenophon came out—until 1973, when appeared his note on the plan of *Beyond Good and Evil*, no one could have guessed that the discoverer of exoteric teaching had not only cleared the path through a *terra incognita* until then, as Strauss said in his famous study *Persecution and the Art of Writing*, but had reached that unknown land through a deeply cultivated field of knowledge. As editor and interpreter of Mendelssohn's writings, Strauss came to feel concerned about the spiritual situation of the enlightened Jew (i.e., the spiritual situation of the modern Jew that could be measured against the Enlightenment and modernity as a whole). The line "Jacobi made public the fact that in Lessing's view there was no philosophy but the philosophy of Spinoza" actually concealed many other lines. Publication, indeed, might not be the best or the only way to make known an opinion that, perhaps, inasmuch as it would be only an opinion, might not be authentic or final, and that in any case, insofar as it would be only an opinion, would always be inferior to knowledge. Philosophy as such, including Spinoza's philosophy, as Strauss repeated on numerous occasions, consists in replacing opinion by knowledge. The fact that Jacobi had made public an opinion on Spinoza did not mean that he knew what Lessing really thought or knew nor that Jacobi himself had reached any knowledge beyond Lessing's opinion about what really mattered; it did not mean either that in the controversy over whether Spinoza's philosophy, and therefore philosophy as such, concealed atheism, Mendelssohn had been closer to the truth in arguing that Lessing had carried out a sort of "purification" of Spinoza's philosophy.[13] Jacobi had dragged Mendelssohn with him to the point that it was no longer possible to think, even in the case of a friend of Lessing, in a "salvation" (*Rettung*). To be saved, Mendelssohn would have had to be able to withstand the spiritual tension created by the critique of modernity and the fight against Plato, but there were no signs of that tension either in his *Phaedo* or in his *Jerusalem*. Mendelssohn was not, as Lessing and Socrates were, a free or ministerial spirit. Recovering the prejudice about the possibility of a premodern philosophy would take Strauss from Moses to Moses (ממשה עד השמ). In his correspondence with Klein, shortly after finishing the last and longest of his introductions to the writings of Mendelssohn, Strauss refers to Maimonides as a free spirit. Maimonides, not Mendelssohn, would be for Strauss the central figure in his studies on the relationship between philosophy and Judaism.[14]

Lessing's case is much more complicated. Lessing was part of Strauss's concern for the relationship between philosophy and Judaism: Lessing had combined Maimonides and Mendelssohn in the character of Nathan.[15] But Nathan was as much a biblical figure as Socrates's modern counterpart: biblical Nathan and classical Socrates prefigure Lessing's Nathan and Lessing himself. Strauss's political philosophy is a meditation on the relationship between philosophy and society—whatever the regime of society might be—whose deepest and most superficial intuition is that all societies, including the ancient city and modern secular society, are conservative.[16] Strauss considered that the controversy over Spinoza's philosophy was, despite what Jacobi had tried to prove, an improvisation by Lessing whose inspiration went back to the Platonic dialogues. In many respects, Lessing, for whom classical sources were as familiar as the reaction that could be expected from the modern public, had opened to Strauss the way to those sources and how to make them known. The fact that the conversation with Jacobi was a dramatic replica or paraphrase of the Platonic dialogues makes us think of Lessing as if Lessing had combined in his character the figures of Socrates and Plato; if Jacobi, not Lessing, was the material reporter of the conversation, then Lessing was given the role of Socrates; the fact that Jacobi (like Mendelssohn) was unable to understand what Lessing had said, made Jacobi into a sophist. Therefore, Jacobi was not Plato. (The *Pantheismusstreit* preceded the chapter in the history of philosophy about the relationship between German idealism and the "theory of ideas.")

In 1971, Leo Strauss wrote to Alexander Altmann, who had resumed the edition of the works of Mendelssohn that had been interrupted by the Nazis, to thank him for his praise of the work that Strauss had conducted thirty-four years earlier in Germany. Lessing, not Mendelssohn, was still the "problem" as Strauss emphasized; not so much the existence of an esoteric doctrine in Lessing, about which Strauss and Altmann agreed, but its hypothetical content. "In 1937," Strauss wrote, "I had meant to present, either in a concluding part of the introduction or in a separate article (under the title *Taking Leave of Germany* [*Abschied von Deutschland*]) the center of Lessing's thoughts *de Deo et mundo*. The decisive points are still as clear to me now as they were then." Strauss's avowal, near the end of his life, that "the only thing I could do was to refer my better students strongly to Lessing" was a proper gesture of a philosopher of the future; that is, of a platonic political philosopher. We can think of Leo Strauss when reading, in Goethe's conversations, that we need another Lessing.[17]

NOTES

1. See Laurence Lampert, *Nietzsche's Task. An Interpretation of Beyond Good and Evil* (New Haven, CT: Yale University Press, 2001), and the earlier *Leo Strauss and Nietzsche* (Chicago: University of Chicago Press, 1996), and also the more recent *The Enduring Importance of Leo Strauss* (Chicago: University of Chicago Press, 2013), 72: "The purpose of my book—showing the enduring importance of Leo Strauss—includes arguing that Nietzsche read the spiritual situation of the present more accurately than Strauss did." The aim of this chapter is to provide, acknowledging the teachings of Lampert—especially his reading of Strauss's correspondence with Jacob Klein and of his writings on Jehuda ha-Levi, Xenophon and, of course, Nietzsche—a counterargument. See aphorism 3 of *Beyond Good and Evil* about "having read between their [the philosophers'] lines long enough" (*Beyond Good and Evil. Prelude to a Philosophy of the Future*, ed. Rolf-P. Horstmann and Judith Norman [Cambridge: Cambridge University Press, 2001], 6). Cf. Nietzsche's "Vorspiel" and the Platonic προοίμιον (*Resp.* 357a, *Legg.* 722c–723c), that Strauss's disciples Allan Bloom and Thomas L. Pangle translate as "prelude" (*The Republic of Plato*, ed. Allan Bloom [New York: Basic Books, 1991], 35, and *The Laws of Plato*, ed. Thomas L. Pangle [Chicago: University of Chicago Press, 1988], 109–110). The Athenian Stranger introduces the proem or prelude at "noon," the time when, as everyone knows, "Incipit Zarathustra."
2. "Das *Maass* ist uns fremd" (moderation is foreign to us); Cf. aphorism 224 in *Beyond Good and Evil*. See Antonio Lastra, "Micrología: Leo Strauss y la historia de la filosofía," in *Tradición e innovación en la historia intelectual. Métodos historiográficos*, ed. Faustino Oncina (Madrid: Biblioteca Nueva, 2013), 131–140.
3. Cf. Plato, *Resp.* 412d–e and 456b–c, and *Genesis* 4:9, 4:17. Plato distinguished between the founders or legislators—that is, "us," the speakers in the dialogue—and the guardians of the city of logos, which would be neither Athens nor the "true" and "healthy" "city of pigs" (cf. *Resp.* 369c and 372d); Cain, who denies being his brother's guardian, is the founder of the Bible's first city. On the relation between πόλις and עיר, between Socrates and Nathan, see the first

two paragraphs of Strauss's "What is Political Philosophy?" (*WIPP*, 9–10), and Leo Strauss, "Jerusalem and Athens: Some Preliminary Reflections," in *SPPP*, 147–173, and particularly 168 and 172. On the contrast between κατὰ φύσιν and παρὰ φύσιν, cf. aphorisms 9, 21, 51, 55, 49, 126, 188, and 197 in *Beyond Good and Evil*. See also Leo Strauss, "The Law of Reason in the *Kuzari*," in *PAW*, 133–141, and Strauss's letter to Gershom Scholem on 22 November 1960: "What you call *nihil*, the falâsifa call *physis*" (*GS 3*, 743).

4. Cf. *Phaedrus* 264b and 275d–276 and the last aphorism of *Beyond Good and Evil*. *Beyond Good and Evil* is not "the only book published by Nietzsche." The phrase is an example of the "deliberate mistakes" of reticent writing. Nietzsche had published the fourth part of *Thus Spoke Zarathustra* in a private edition. In the poem that follows the last aphorism of *Beyond Good and Evil* (that is, the final expression of the beauty of the book), Nietzsche refers to the arrival of Zarathustra. Nietzsche calls it "From high mountains"; in Platonic terms, however, this would mean a descent from philosophy to poetry.
5. See the preface and aphorism 289 in *Beyond Good and Evil*, and Leo Strauss, "Note on the plan of Nietzsche's *Beyond Good and Evil*," in *SPPP*, 174–191. Compare the first sentence in the "Note" in connection with *ipsissimosität* and its relation to eternity with the first sentence in "Xenophon's *Anabasis*": "*Beyond Good and Evil* always seemed to me to be the most beautiful of Nietzsche's books"; "Xenophon's *Anabasis* seems today to be regarded universally as his most beautiful book" (*SPPP*, 174, 105). Both the note on *Beyond Good and Evil* and the study on the *Anabasis* are posthumous, although Strauss decided where they should have been placed in *SPPP*: between an essay on the gods in Thucydides's works and a study on natural law in Xenophon's case and between the study on Jerusalem and Athens and a note about Maimonides's *The Book of Knowledge* in Nietzsche. The "Note on the Plan of Nietzsche's *Beyond Good and Evil*" lies at the very heart of the book—the eighth of fifteen studies—where, according to Strauss, are to be found the most important lessons that an author wants to convey. See Joseph Cropsey's preface (*SPPP*, vii) and Laurence Lampert, *The Enduring Importance of Leo Strauss*, 311–314. Concerning the unnatural cave

and the natural cave, see *PL*, 25, 135–136n2. On the relationship between Nietzschean and Platonic caves, see Hans Blumenberg, *Höhlenausgänge* (Frankfurt am Main: Suhrkamp, 1989), VI, v.

6. "How a city can take philosophy in hand without being destroyed," as Bloom literally translates (*The Republic of Plato*, 177 [497d]). διολεῖται corresponds to διαβολὴν (497a), that Bloom accurately translates as "slandered": philosophy has been falsely accused, slandered, referring to the trial of Socrates. See the obscure passage of 496, with reference to the "flight" (ὑπὸ φυγῆς καταληφθὲν, "held in check by exile") and the reluctance of Socrates (τὸ δ' ἡμέτερον οὐκ ἄξιον λέγειν, τὸ δαιμόνιον σημεῖον), that prefigure the Athenian Stranger of the *Laws*. See *AAPL*, and "A Giving of Accounts" (1970), in *JPCM*, 457–466: "Without cities, no philosophers. They are the conditions." (Leo Strauss)
7. See the "ministerial" nature of the interpreter's mediation in Strauss's correspondence with Hans-Georg Gadamer (CCWM) and the "ministerial" nature of poetry in relation to Platonic political philosophy with the *complementärer Mensch*, whom Nietzsche identified with the philosopher (Laurence Lampert, *The Enduring Importance of Leo Strauss*, 128–155, 300–307).
8. Cf. *Resp.* 607b and *OPS*, 119–142. See *TM* and *SA*.
9. Cf. aphorism 44 in *Beyond Good and Evil* and paragraph 5 of the "Note on the Plan of Nietzsche's *Beyond Good and Evil*." See the preface and the first aphorism of the second volume of *Human, all too human: A book for free spirits*—of which Nietzsche published the second edition in the same year as *Beyond Good and Evil*—about those "disappointed in philosophy" (*Enttäuschten der Philosophie*).
10. See "An Introduction to Heideggerian Existentialism," in *RCPP*, 40–41.
11. See "Why We Remain Jews" (1962), in *JPCM*, 311–356 (particularly page 333, where Strauss mentions Lessing during the debate after his lecture). In the conclusion to a lecture Strauss gave in 1948 invited by Karl Löwith, which he wouldn't publish afterwards, Strauss paid homage not to "the Lessing of a certain tradition, the Lessing celebrated by a certain type of oratory, but the true and unknown Lessing" (RR, 178).

12. About Strauss's "change of orientation," see "Preface to the English Translation" (1965), in *SCR*, 31 (*LAM*, 257), and *Reorientation: Leo Strauss in the 1930s*, ed. Martin D. Yaffe and Richard S. Ruderman (New York: Palgrave Macmillan, 2014).
13. On Mendelssohnian "purification" of Spinoza's philosophy understood as pantheism rather than atheism see Strauss's introduction to *Morning hours* and *To the friends of Lessing* in *LSMM*, 59–145, and also Yaffe's interpretative essay (219–317). Strauss's introductions to Mendelssohn's texts have been published in the original German in *GS 2*, 465–606. Cf. Apollonian "purification," *Resp*. 399e.
14. "Maimonides wird immer aufregender. Er war ein wirklich freier Geist" (letter to Klein on January 20, 1938, written in the United States, in *GS 3*, 545). Shortly before, in the preliminary remark to what was to be an essay about Lessing, Strauss had justified the choice of a Christian such as Lessing in the fact that "despite searching in earnest among the apostate or suspect Jews of modern times, he found not one man with Lessing's intellectual freedom [*der geistigen Freiheit*]" ("Eine Erinnerung an Lessing," *GS 2*, 607–608; *LSMM*, 161). See *LSMC* and Kenneth Hart Green, *Leo Strauss and the Rediscovery of Maimonides* (Chicago: University of Chicago Press, 2013). The three notes on Maimonides in *SPPP*—Strauss's last words on Maimonides—can be found between the note on Nietzsche and a chapter on Machiavelli.
15. A historical essay on Nathan the Wise, preceded by another on *Pantheismusstreit*—a chapter in the history of philosophy to whose understanding Strauss contributed in a way that was important as it was relatively unknown until recently—would have been the last one of those which composed the first book that Strauss intended to publish in the United States. See "Appendix 1: Plan of a Book Tentatively Entitled *Philosophy and the Law: Historical Essays*," in *JPCM*, 467–470.
16. See SSTX, 502–536:

> For it would be an overstatement to say that philosophy was compatible with Athens: Socrates was executed for not believing in the gods of Athens, in the gods of the city. By considering and reconsidering this fact, we grasp the

> ultimate reason why political life and philosophic life, even if compatible for almost all practical purposes, are incompatible in the last analysis: political life, if taken seriously, meant belief in the gods of the city, and philosophy is the denial of the gods of the city.

Strauss did not include this essay—the first on classic issues—in any of his books. Its publication was parallel to the appearance of his first work on Maimonides in English, a review of "The first book of Maimonides's *Mišnèh Tôrāh*" (see *LSMC*, 329–340), and to the writing of "Exoteric teaching," that Strauss didn't publish either (see ET, 275–292).

17. Cf. *Gespräche mit Goethe*, 15 October 1825. See Alexander Altmann's preliminary notice to the Mendelssohn volume that Strauss had prepared in Moses Mendelssohn, *Gesammelte Schriften Jubiläumsausgabe* (Stuttgart-Bad Cannstaat: Friedrich Fromman Verlag/Günther Holzboog, 1974) 3/2, vii–ix (in English in *LSMM*, 3–5). Strauss is referring to the same text he had entitled "Eine Erinnerung an Lessing" in 1937 in which he wrote that he "was not undmindful of the obligation of thanks owed by his *nation* [i.e., the Jewish nation] to that great son of the German nation, especially at this moment of farewell" (*LSMM*, 162). Strauss corrected *Abschieds* and wrote *Trennung* instead. The farewell or parting from Germany recalls the Nietzschean or Platonic flight of Lessing and Leo Strauss.

Philosophy and History of Philosophy

Carlo Altini

In a passage of the *Moralia*, Plutarch tells a story by Antiphanes of Chio, about Plato's followers:

> Antiphanes recounted, jokingly, that in a certain city it was so cold that as soon as words were spoken they froze, and that later, when they thawed, the inhabitants heard in the summer what had been said in the winter. The same thing happened to Plato's teachings to his followers when they were still young, and so later and with difficulty most of them only understood when they were old. This typically happens with philosophy in general.[1]

In recalling this anecdote, Plutarch was perhaps thinking of philosophy as a lifestyle, but certainly he was not thinking of the contemporary idea of the history of philosophy that was only possible in the post-Hegelian era. It is not obvious that philosophy has a history: before Hegel there were, at most, biographies of philosophers and lists compiling the opinions of philosophers. (There thus exists an introduction to philosophy without philosophical value.) But there is no history of philosophy with *philosophical significance* for philosophy. The relationship between philosophy and the history of philosophy is very different from that of the history of science with science itself: even without taking into account the theoretical difficulty associated with the recognition of philosophy as an object of historical research, the history of philosophy cannot be a philosophical paleontology or a history of progress of the human mind.

Naturally it would be simplistic to try and resolve the problem of the philosophical meaning of the relationship between philosophy and the history of philosophy without having defined what is intended by "philosophy" (or its essence) on one hand, and the "history of philosophy" (or its object) on the other. All this had direct implications for the activities, for example, of philosophical historiography and philosophical hermeneutics. This simple observation demonstrates how wide-ranging and difficult the task is (which, in reflecting on the philosophical meaning of the history of philosophy, would have to take into account the conflicting interpretations of Hegel and Dilthey, Heidegger and Collingwood, Croce and Gramsci, Gentile and Dewey, Gadamer and Garin). It is also important to note the underlying issue that characterizes the problem of the history of philosophy: the historical scholar of philosophy has to consider the philosophical value of the doctrines of the past, but at the same time cannot attribute to any of these doctrines an absolute degree of truth, on pain of straying outside the bounds of good practice of a historian.

Here evidence emerges of a further difficulty regarding the relationship between history (understood as the search for transitory and particular truths) and philosophy (understood as the search for unchanging universal truths): the historical method, looking for the originality and unusual nature of a fact, is inadequate for achieving the objectives of the history of philosophy, nor can it provide the key for achieving conciliation between history and philosophy. History is different from philosophy, and in a certain sense history and philosophy are exact opposites: history seeks to reveal particular truths while philosophy seeks to reveal universal truths. The expression "history of philosophy" thus appears contradictory.

How is it possible to define a history of philosophy? It is undoubtedly possible to compile a history of the lives of philosophers, just as it is possible to write a history of philosophies: the first is a classic genre, doxography, while the second involves writing a history of philosophical theories, but understood as opinions rather than as the outcomes of research into truth. It is not possible, however, to write a history of the various philosophies understood as "truths." How could it be possible to consider as philosophical truths the elaborations of both Aquinas and Hobbes, or Aristotle and Spinoza? The task might be more accessible if we consider philosophy as a *search* for truth, without attributing a progressive significance to this search process. However, this embodies a hidden contradiction, because a history of philosophy constitutes a philosophical problem that has as object not existence nor the world, but the philosophy itself, which calls into question the pretext of universality through the subjectification of what, by its very nature, claims to be objective, or philosophical truth.

Facing this problem, Hegel resorted to the idea of a nonsubjective history 'resolving' the history of philosophy in philosophy, thereby destroying the historicity itself of the philosophical systems. Collingwood, like many other idealist authors close to the historicist tradition, opted for the idea of a radical historical conditionality of philosophy: philosophy is historical because humankind is historical. Historicity is the condition of possibility of philosophical discourse. Other philosophers such as Plato or Descartes would have been radically critical of this approach, since for them philosophy is a discourse on truth unconditioned by history. Regardless of these opposing solutions, there nevertheless remains a complex relationship between philosophy and historicity: philosophical knowledge, when it acts, appears to act in only a *mediated* way, considering that philosophy prepares an investigation that is essentially and necessarily noncurrent, and which, as in the anecdote of Antiphanes of Chio narrated by Plutarch, sees its meaning realized in the future. Philosophy remains a form of knowledge that not only refuses temporal localization but subjects time to its own scale, both past and future. Philosophy is essentially noncurrent: it belongs to that class of things destined never to achieve an immediate impact in the present.

1. HISTORY OF PHILOSOPHY AND HISTORICISM

Strauss began addressing the history of political philosophy in the 1920s and 1930s, dedicating himself to the study of the conflict between modern philosophy, premodern philosophy, and Judaism clearly represented in the *Theological-Political Treatise* by Spinoza.[2] The motivation for this decision was not academic curiosity, but rather a response to the "crisis of values" that was enveloping the entire European culture. After the collapse of all the philosophical systems, the scenario for a young German–Jewish philosopher in the Weimar Republic was certainly not reassuring: it is enough to mention the names of Nietzsche and Spengler to epitomize the spiritual climate pervading German culture during these years. It was a climate dominated by an awareness of the crisis in meaning and the role of science and politics in the modern world, a struggle between nihilism and rationalization and reification, *Kultur* and *Zivilisation*. In this sense it is not possible to define the 'return' of Strauss to premodern philosophy (of Plato and Maimonides in particular) as a form of nostalgia or refuge in the past, because he was perfectly aware that a direct and immediate recovery of classic political philosophy was impossible: as necessary as this recovery might be, it could be no more than experimental. It was not the concrete political solutions offered by the classics—which are not directly applicable to the problems posed by modern societies—that had to be recovered, but rather the forms of classical philosophical-political thought. The motivation that drove Strauss to the recovery of the ancients against the moderns is thus ultramodern and dictated by the need to overcome the crisis in the modern world (obvious, for example, in the horror of the drift towards totalitarianism and the relativism of liberal outlooks).

Historical reflection is a necessary means to overcome the problems of modernity: Strauss studied Plato and Machiavelli, Xenophon and Hobbes, Maimonides and Spinoza, Aristophanes and Locke, Thucydides and Rousseau in an attempt to overcome the contradictions in the modern experiment, brought clearly into focus by Nietzsche. The reconstruction of the philosophies of the authors of the past is therefore not only presented as research of a historical nature, aiming to identify the truths of the past, but also as a sort of return to the roots of modernity through a deconstruction of modern political philosophy. In this way historical research, historical reconstruction, and theoretical thought turn out to be inseparable: Strauss's questions about modernity are born out of reflection on the contemporary crisis and are developed through the acquisition of historical critical instruments with the aim of arriving at a new understanding of the current situation. If historical research aims to be more than simply a collection of sources and scholarly materials, it needs close comparison with philosophical research which, in turn, historically acts by the reconstruction of certain texts of the past, tracing out lines of dialogue and genealogical trees between philosophers that outline new historiographic paths of philosophical relevance.[3]

In order to understand the relationships between philosophy and the history of philosophy in Strauss's thought, his antihistorical argument (also elaborated according to the principles of his hermeneutic), through which history, philosophy, and historicism are distinguished, must be taken into account. History is a form of scientific-narrative knowledge that examines the facts and ideas of the past. Philosophy is a form of knowledge that aims to understand 'what is.' Historicism is a particular interpretation of philosophical knowledge, in which all philosophical and scientific knowledge is historical knowledge. History thus represents a knowledge that seeks the truth of what is particular; philosophy is a knowledge that seeks the truth of what is universal; historicism is instead an attempt to define philosophy as historically conditioned knowledge, incapable of achieving truth. According to Strauss there also exists a clear difference between historicism thus defined and the history of philosophy, which is a type of knowledge that aims to reconstruct forms and contents of the philosophies of the past and that has the potential of achieving the truth. Philosophy and the history of philosophy are obviously not the same thing; but nevertheless the history of philosophy may fulfil certain aims and functions of philosophy, especially in times of crisis: indeed, the idea itself of a history of philosophy presupposes that certain fundamental philosophical problems persist through the ages.

The distortion between history and philosophy caused by historicism therefore poses a problem of knowledge both to history and to philosophy. A problem of inadequacy of the sources of historical information is transformed into a problem of theoretical knowledge, in particular as regards the statute of philosophical activity. Vice versa, the inadequacy of the form of theoretical knowledge available makes it difficult, if not impossible, to achieve an adequate historical understanding of philosophical activities in past eras. It therefore becomes necessary, according to Strauss, to establish what the differences are between the fundamental characteristics of correct historical research and the philosophical principles of historicism, in order to recover the distinction between historical issues and philosophical issues, abandoning the idea of a universal philosophical history. If philosophy is not determined by historicity or localization, but from its nature, the subject of historical research (within its philosophical relevance) is not to identify the historical-social energy that would have determined the conditions of possibility and the objectives of the philosophical discourse that, in this sense, would be reduced to a mere ideological product of material conditions. The subject of historical research is instead to reread the texts of the philosophical tradition and to identify the philosophical turning points in the tradition. In the analysis of philosophical texts, the task of a correct historical research becomes to eliminate rigid historically deterministic suppositions, with related psychological and socio-economic reductionisms, in favor of a purely philosophical assessment of the texts and their reciprocal dialogue. In Strauss's view the history of philosophy is a plane marked by a radical discontinuity between ancient and modern, but it is also a unifying plane since it is characterized by the permanence of concepts and categories, concretely visible in the critical dialogue between the classics. In this way only is it possible to safeguard the autonomy of philosophy while defending the universal nature of philosophical thought from relativism and ideology.

2. FROM SOCIAL POSITIVISM TO HISTORICISM

In Strauss's interpretation, historicism is the final outcome of the modern crisis. The highest exponent of historicism is Martin Heidegger but, as regards the relationship between philosophy and the history of philosophy, Strauss criticizes Robin George Collingwood. However, as an introduction to Strauss's criticism of Collingwood, it is important to understand its place within a wider discussion of the relativism of modern philosophy, exemplified in the transition from social positivism (Max Weber) to historicism. For Strauss the task assumed by modern science resides in the replacement of the image of reality derived from common sense with a scientific image of reality. The problem derives from the conflict of two opposite forms of scepticism: the ancient-Medieval on one hand (represented by Plato and Maimonides), and modern scepticism on the other hand that ranges from Descartes to Hegel through Hume and Kant, ending up in the contemporary nihilistic expressions, obvious in Nietzsche and Heidegger. In the Straussian interpretation, the radical distinction between natural image and scientific image, founded on the criterion of radical doubt, leads to inverse results compared to those reached following Socratic scepticism, keeping in mind that that the search for wisdom requires a dialectic path through contradictory common opinions. By rendering the model of scientific understanding independent of the model of natural perception, Cartesian scepticism is nothing other than a modern form of dogmatism: the central problem of Descartes in *Meditations* consists in an attempt to construct a new metaphysical foundation for science.

Modern philosophy and modern science construct an image of reality through a particular modification of the real, such as to surpass natural understanding, considered as a hybrid generated from a mingling of the subjective world of sensations and the objective world of external reality. Modern scientific knowledge is radically distinct from natural or prescientific knowledge and comes about from a radical transformation—not an improvement—of the latter. In this way the world in which we live is no longer the natural world, but a product of modern science. An epistemological approach of this type leads to a relativistic shift from philosophy to history and sociology, especially through the definition of rules and institutions of direct effectiveness and practical applicability, with the reduction of political philosophy to techniques on one hand (as in the legal positivism of Hans Kelsen) and to ideology on the other hand (as in the decisionism of Carl Schmitt).

Strauss's argument is mostly directed against the two fundamental currents of philosophical thought of the 1800s, social positivism and historicism. In the Straussian interpretation, in particular in *What is Political Philosophy?*, the modern distinction between scientific knowledge and natural knowledge generates the idea that scientific knowledge is unable to take value judgments into account. This idea leads the way to an ethically neutral political philosophy founded on the conviction that there is a radical difference between facts and value judgments, and that only factual judgments fall within the realm of social science. The outcomes of such a social science are catastrophic: knowledge becomes instrumental, at the service of all purposes regardless of their noble or evil nature.

Strauss identifies Max Weber as the primary representative of a social positivism that transforms itself progressively into historicism. For Weber a historical process does not have meaning apart from the subjective meanings present in the actions of individual actors: the propositions of positivistic social science thus comprise the answers to questions that depend on the orientation of the interests of the social scientist or of the society to which he or she belongs, in particular on his concepts of value. The objects of the social sciences are provided by a "reference to values": but, since the reference to values is inextricably linked to the contingent situation, social science is linked to history. In Strauss's interpretation of Weber, it is thus impossible to speak of a "natural frame of reference" or a "definitive system of fundamental concepts" because all frames of reference are changeable, considering that no socio-cultural order can be defined as the right or rational order. Social reality is in itself an infinite and meaningless process of individual events infinitely divisible: within this framework the underlying problems, and thus the questions that social science must answer, change with the shifting historical and cultural context. An evaluative study of facts presupposes a selection of the relevant questions guided by an orientation based on values, in turn determined by a historical selection from among the values that underlie the conceptual scheme within which the social scientist operates. In the Straussian interpretation social science provides scientific answers to nonscientific questions since the questions are formulated from the perspective of the present and start from historically contingent ideas of value.

However, Strauss believed that Weber never demonstrated the theoretical difference between facts and values; that is, their assumed absolute heterogeneity: it had never been demonstrated that the conflict between values is an irresolvable issue for human reason, given that such a demonstration would require a comprehensive critique of the criteria of evaluation. A consequence of the heterogeneity of facts and values is the impossibility of reaching conclusions about values starting from facts, and vice versa: social science can answer questions regarding facts and their causes but is unqualified to answer questions regarding values. Social science is by nature ethically neutral: there is a fundamental difference between reference to a value (which implies a rational analysis) and judgment of the value (which is essentially irrational). Social scientists who identify a link between an object and the protection of liberty do not necessarily assume a position in favor of liberty, nor provide an evaluation of the object, instead limiting themselves to identifying the causal connections. Ethical imperatives and cultural values are subjective, so much so that it is impossible for the reason to scientifically justify a noble ideal rather than an ignoble ideal: the choice between the different ends can be made in full awareness of causes, choosing the most suitable means to achieve the predefined ends; but this cannot be in itself rational, because reason cannot say which ends must be preferred to others. Not by chance the dignity of people consists in freedom, in autonomy interpreted as capacity to define their own final values (their own demon) and to choose rationally the appropriate means to match these values. Such a position—which brings together relativism and nihilism—was unacceptable to Strauss:

> Weber contended that his notion of a "value-free" or ethically neutral social science is fully justified by what he regarded as the most fundamental of all oppositions, namely, the opposition of the Is and the Ought, or the opposition of reality and norm or value. But the conclusion from the radical heterogeneity of the Is and the Ought to the impossibility of an evaluating social science is obviously not valid. Let us assume that we had genuine knowledge of right and wrong, or of the Ought, or of the true value system. That knowledge, while not derived

> from empirical science, would legitimately direct all empirical social science; it would be the foundation of all empirical social science. For social science is meant to be of practical value. It tries to find means for given ends. For this purpose it has to understand the ends. Regardless of whether the ends are "given" in a different manner from the means, the end and the means belong together; therefore, "the end belongs to the same science as the means" (Aristotle, *Physics*, 194a26–27). If there were genuine knowledge of the ends, that knowledge would naturally guide all search for means. There would be no reason to delegate knowledge of the ends to social philosophy and the search for the means to an independent social science. Based on genuine knowledge of the true ends, social science would search for the proper means to those ends; it would lead up to objective and specific value judgments regarding policies. Social science would be a truly policy-making, not to say architectonic, science rather than a mere supplier of data for the real policy-makers. The true reason why Weber insisted on the ethically neutral character of social science as well as of social philosophy was, then, not his belief in the fundamental opposition of the Is and the Ought but his belief that there cannot be any genuine knowledge of the Ought. He denied to man any science, empirical or rational, any knowledge, scientific or philosophic, of the true value system: the true value system does not exist; there is a variety of values which are of the same rank, whose demands conflict with one another, and whose conflict cannot be solved by human reason. Social science or social philosophy can do no more than clarify that conflict and all its implications; the solution has to be left to the free, nonrational decision of each individual.[4]

Strauss contests the stance of Weberian social science on all fronts: with reference to the Kantian horizon of "must be," he revealed its philosophical weakness; in relation to its dependence on historicism, he revealed its scientific inconsistency; as regards the relationship between facts and values, he established its lack of ethical weight;

finally, in relation to his concrete work as interpreter of the sociology of religions, he revealed its contradictory nature, to the extent of indicating the Weberian methodological principles as an obstacle to his own historical-social research. Indeed, everything that Weber had strived to expunge from sociological theory—in particular the possibility of passing value judgments—comes into play in his works dedicated to the analysis of individual religious ethics, in which it is essential, for example, to distinguish between ethos and living techniques, between religion and superstition, between religious conviction and liturgical formalism, and so on. Weber insisted in the conviction that the conflict between values and ethical choices cannot be resolved by reason because there are no objective rules and there is no hierarchy of values: for Strauss, however, this conviction had not been demonstrated by Weber, but only postulated on the basis of his moral preference (which Strauss identified as the Weberian preference for conflict rather than peace). Furthermore, by following the Weberian methodology, the social scientist arrives at the point of no longer being able to justify his or her own philosophical or scientific activity, because it is no longer based on obvious suppositions but on a decision without foundation, on a preference in relation to the search for truth perceived as a value, not as a fact: in Strauss's view of Weber, science and philosophy are not capable of perceiving their own basis because the search for truth is a value that can be chosen or rejected. Social science can thus not avoid issuing value judgments on social behavior, but under the handicap of not being able to formulate prescriptions, even descriptions of social structures. Indeed, it is impossible to study societies without referring to their aims, which thus serve as precepts for the judgment of the societies themselves.

Social science can avoid value judgments only if it surrenders to the interpretations (and thus the falsifications) those social subjects provide for themselves: but such a social science is pointless—because it inhibits any form of critical awareness—as well as being dangerous, since it justifies, at least on a methodological level, any moral inclination and more generally, conformism. A refusal of value judgments puts the objectivity of historical-social research at risk: research that aims to understand the social actors in the way that they understand themselves is undoubtedly useful and fertile, but only if it is preparatory to a critical interpretation from which value judgments are not excluded. This type of social science is conformist by nature because, within its theoretical construction, it cannot but level itself with the reference values of the present society, which cannot be called into discussion. Political philosophy thus loses its critical potential and its inclination for truth, instead limiting itself to an instrumental dimension available to every power here and now. The conception of values as dependent on society implies their dependence on history: the objective answers of science draw their meaning from subjective questions; that is, from the specific interests of the subject and not from logic, so that science itself is demonstrated to be historical:

> One must conceive of the values embodied in a given social science as dependent on the society to which the social science in question belongs, *i.e.* on history. Not only is social science superseded by historical studies; social science itself proves to be "historical" [. . .]. It is only at this point that we come face to face with the serious antagonist of political philosophy: historicism. After having reached its full growth, historicism is distinguished from positivism by the following characteristics. 1) It abandons the distinction between facts and values, because every understanding, however theoretical, implies specific evaluations. 2) It denies the authoritative character of modern science, which appears as only one form among many of man's thinking orientation in the world. 3) It refuses to regard the historical process as fundamentally progressive, or as rational.[5]

Historical understanding becomes the basis for empirical science and society, and the categories of theoretical understanding imply principles of evaluation that are historically determined: social positivism is thus transformed into historicism, abandoning the distinction between facts and values, simply because every theoretical understanding implies specific evaluations. The refusal of the idea of a 'good life' is the necessary consequence of the short circuit between philosophical relativism and scientific absolutism: due to the essentially historical nature of human thought, philosophy gives way to *Weltanschauungslehre*. In the view of the historicism of the period there can be no natural knowledge through which philosophy becomes possible, understood as the search for truth, and consequently natural rights. But in the Straussian interpretation, philosophy (in the Platonic tense of the term), and thus natural right, cannot exist unless there is an absolute horizon that does not change through the changes of history: for historicism and social positivism instead there is a historical-cultural multiplicity of principles of the good and right that reciprocally contradict each other and that cannot demonstrate their superiority or justify their foundations.

3. AGAINST COLLINGWOOD

Strauss widely contested the modern confusion between history and philosophy, which was the origin of the various versions of contemporary historicism, especially in his long discussion of the book *The Idea of History* (1946) by Collingwood. In this discussion clearly emerge the affinities between different formulations of scientific history, epistemology of history, and philosophy of history, all closely linked to the reformulation of the historic nature of modern philosophy, in which there is the implicit idea that thought is historically conditioned. The point of view of the historian—but also of the scientist and the philosopher—is thus without universal or objective validity, given that the philosophical thought of every era, being essentially an expression of the spirit of the times, is equally true, every form of knowledge is uniquely relative and present, and, above all, every truth is valid only within its own historical period. The main subject of historicism assumes the existence of a plurality of planes of historical-cultural reference, all equally legitimate; so every form of theoretical understanding presupposes a specific plane of historical reference within which it lies. Nevertheless, precisely because, if one starts from the experience of history, any form of teaching can be justified, so the argument of historicism cannot be founded on a historical experience, but on a philosophical analysis that demonstrates the essential and "natural" changeableness of the categories of thought. But in the Straussian interpretation, it is precisely this lack of demonstration that historicism exhibits, in a self-contradictory manner, its own metahistorical and dogmatic nature: by imposing the basic historicity of thought, historicism confirms its own historicity, and so the provisional nature of its own validity. At the very moment in which the historicist sustains the metahistorical truth of his or her own theses, he or she admits, contradicting these theses, that thought can achieve a universally valid truth: the argumentation is thus founded on a particular interpretation of philosophical knowledge, certainly not justified but only masked, by the historical data on which this interpretation is based. According to Strauss it is necessary to carefully verify the characteristics of historical research implicit in Collingwood's philosophical position, precisely because there is a fatal gap between historical research and historicism:

> The same belief, which forced [Collingwood] to attempt to become a historian of thought, prevented him from becoming a historian of thought. He was forced to attempt to become a historian of thought because he believed that to know the human mind is to know its history, or that self-knowledge is historical understanding. But this belief contradicts the tacit premise of all earlier thought, that premise being the view that to know the human mind is something fundamentally different from knowing the history of the human mind. Collingwood therefore rejected the thought of the past as untrue in the decisive respect. Hence he could not take that thought seriously, for to take a thought seriously means to regard it as possible that the thought in question is true. He therefore lacked the incentive for re-enacting the thought of the past: he did not re-enact the thought of the past.[6]

In Strauss's view, Collingwood's philosophy of history is not just epistemology of history but, above all, metaphysics of history: the apparent relativism present in the consideration of the historically conditioned character of every thought turns out to be, on the contrary, a form of imperialistic dogmatism. The historical understanding rendered possible in the present is, for the modern historian such as Collingwood, superior both to the historical understanding possible in the past and to the way that the thought of the past interpreted itself, given that the thought of the past can be known only through the method of re-enactment, or in other words through a form of criticism. The thought of the past is thus studied starting from a historical supposition (simultaneously relativistic and dogmatic) that is completely extraneous to the thought itself. In the Straussian interpretation, the philosophy of history of Collingwood aims, through the organic unity of the total experience of the modern historian, to the accumulation of knowledge that tends to form a universal philosophical history in which the materials provided by the past are understood and assessed from the privileged perspective of the present. The result resides in the legitimization of the idea of progress and in the creation of a perspective model of history, linked only to a specific tradition—here and now—that, due to a lack of interest in difference, is unable to understand the specific nature of facts and ideas of the past. In this sense the opposition between nonhistorical classical philosophy and modern historical philosophy brings to light the inversion in the relationship between history and philosophy, characterized by the abandonment of the distinction between philosophical problems and historical problems. By reformulating the historical character of modern philosophy, Collingwood had transformed philosophical issues into historical issues relative to the future. To escape from the prison of historical subjectivity, unjustified from a philosophical perspective, it is instead necessary, according to Strauss, to abandon the attempt to understand the past in the light of the present. Collingwood sustains that it is possible to understand authors better than authors can understand themselves. However, this understanding, that claims to be the true understanding, is marked by a clearly antihistorical prejudice.

In Strauss's view historical understanding is an interpretive reconstruction through which it is possible to understand the way in which authors of the past understood themselves. We cannot be seriously interested in the past if we consider that the present is superior to the past: whatever the reason for addressing historical and historiographic issues, we must at least provisionally accept the coordinates applied by the thinkers of the past and attempt to understand them within their original, authentic meaning before formulating critical assessments of them. In this sense, understanding must precede criticism. Historians of philosophy must not substitute their own ideas for those of the authors they are interpreting and must not presume to judge them before understanding them: making a history of philosophy means, for Strauss, attempting to recover lost forms of knowledge. It is possible to recover areas of objectivity in historical research and it is possible to understand correctly the texts of the authors of the past, as they intended them. If they do not want to confuse arbitrarily criticism and interpretation, the historians of thought must preliminarily subordinate their own issues to the issues that their sources sought to resolve. Naturally Strauss is aware that every interpretation is a form of criticism: the choice itself of a specific theme, author, or text considered relevant is a critical act that precedes interpretation. Nevertheless, interpretation and criticism are not the same thing: they are not only distinguishable but also separable. Interpretation necessarily precedes criticism:

> History as history, as quest for the understanding of the past, necessarily presupposes that our understanding of the past is incomplete. The criticism which is inseparable from interpretation is fundamentally different from the criticism which would coincide with the complete understanding. If we call "interpretation" that understanding or criticism which remains within the limits of Plato's own directives, and if we call "criticism" that understanding or criticism which disregards Plato's directives, we may say that interpretation necessarily precedes criticism because the quest for understanding necessarily precedes completed understanding and therewith the judgment which coincides with the completed understanding.[7]

Historians of philosophy must have an initial act of loyalty in relation to the object of study, because they must take into account the real possibility of learning something of important philosophical relevance from the study of the thinkers of the past, rather than from the study of the thinkers of the present. It is possible to understand the philosophy of the past if one is willing to learn something not only about the philosophers of the past, but also from them: in some cases a study of classical texts represents the sole possibility for recovering knowledge of fundamental philosophical problems. This possibility becomes a concrete reality in the present era, characterized in Strauss's view by a profound intellectual crisis of the West, the solution for which required a form of emancipation from modern philosophy. Furthermore, the history of philosophy itself is a product of the modern world, which assumed philosophical relevance only after Hegel: in this sense, historians of philosophy have not only the responsibility for the accuracy and objectiveness of their research, but also and above all the responsibility to bring to light the extended duration or indeed permanence of philosophical issues, the question of truth. Historical understanding cannot avoid facing up to the philosophical question: the most important issue always remains philosophical truth, so much so that historians of philosophy must convert themselves to philosophy keeping clearly in mind the philosophical relevance of their historical studies, in view of the rediscovery of the fundamental philosophical issues:

> History has the further task of explaining why the proper understanding of the fundamental problems has become lost in such a manner that the loss presents itself at the outset as a progress. If it is true that loss of understanding of the fundamental problems culminates in the historicization of philosophy or in historicism, the second function of history consists in making intelligible the modern notion of "History" through the understanding of its genesis. Historicism sanctions the loss, or the oblivion, of the natural horizon of human thought by denying the permanence of the fundamental problems. It is the existence of that natural horizon which makes possible "objectivity" and therefore in particular "historical objectivity."[8]

This criticism of modern subjectivity is not extraneous to the Straussian analysis of logical positivism which, rejecting the Kantian a priori and every form of pure intellect, cannot but find itself involved in psychology and in the empirical genesis of science based on what determines its range of possibilities.[9] Positivistic science is not autonomous because its hypotheses, its imagination, and its results depend on external conditions—social, environmental, cultural—that science itself does not generate. Furthermore, science is a necessary activity of a specific human organism that needs to understand causal relations. Without doubt logical positivism attempts to consider science as autonomous, thanks to the distinction between 'origins' and 'validity': nevertheless it does not succeed, according to Strauss, also because it refuses the possibility of making rational judgments of value. But the opinion that value judgments are not subject to rational control encourages the inclination to make irresponsible affirmations regarding right and wrong, good and bad. All this, basically, is caused by the radical reformulation of modern philosophy as a historical philosophy that claims, contrary to classical philosophy, to possess the status of science, radically distinguishing the how from the why.

For Strauss, instead, the possibility of philosophy and of political philosophy in particular, is an eternal opportunity, not tied to the dimension of here and now, for the confrontation of human life and politics. Political philosophy has the task of rendering explicit the attempt that every political action implicitly contains within itself: the attempt to know what is good and what is bad for the political community (and not simply to have opinions). The political philosopher is, in fact, primarily interested in finding the truth. Political philosophy, as a part of philosophy, is research for—not knowledge of—the truth in political issues: given the incapacity to achieve full understanding of everything, people are at least capable of grasping the fundamental issues, of recognizing what each knows and does not know. In this collocation as a borderland between research into truth and opinions, political philosophy is obliged to take into account the beliefs that characterize the life of a community. Opinions and beliefs necessarily conflict with the philosophical search for truth, which is an essentially transpolitical activity: philosophy is the attempt to replace opinions with knowledge, but opinions are the foundation of political life. Strauss underlines, against all conciliatory traditions, the gap between philosophy and politics. Strauss often recalls Plato's definition of the greatest enemy of philosophy: the greatest sophist is the people of the city; that is, the political society. The only discourse politically pronounceable is thus far from the only philosophically true discourse, because philosophy is a discourse on the truth that exists outside of the Platonic cave.

4. HERMENEUTICS, PHILOSOPHY, AND HISTORY OF PHILOSOPHY

Throughout his life Strauss read classical texts: from Spinoza to Maimonides, Plato to Hobbes, Xenophon to Machiavelli. His studies included an analysis of the forms in which these texts were written. From this point of view, it would be correct to define his work as a history of political philosophy, although it needs to be remembered that his historical research was not limited to the characteristic themes of scholarly literature, instead extending across the theoretical areas of reflection addressing all the main categories of political philosophy. Most of Strauss's scientific production is imbued with an unusual copresence of philosophical reflections, hermeneutic investigations, and historical reconstructions, filtered by his arguments against positivism and historicism. Strauss appears to philosophize by minutely reconstructing the structure of certain texts from the past, tracing lines of dialogue and genealogical links between philosophers that set out new historiographic pathways. At the same time his way of constructing the history of philosophy is clearly founded on a specific conception of philosophical activity. The understanding of the relationships between philosophy and the history of philosophy in the thought of Strauss cannot thus be separated from a reflection on his conception of hermeneutics (with particular reference to reticence in philosophical writings), in a radical distinction between history and historicism.

More than in "Persecution and the Art of Writing" (1941), it is in "The Literary Character of the *Guide for the Perplexed*" (1941) that Strauss elaborates his hermeneutic approach together with a successful formulation of a correct methodology for historical research, raising the issue of reticence in principle. In this essay Strauss's work consists essentially in setting down a series of interpretative instruments that permit penetration through the numerous esoteric schemes of the

Guide for the Perplexed by Maimonides. This explains his great attention to the contradictions, silences, ambiguities, and repetitions in the text, with the aim of defining in the smallest detail and without any reference to any mystical or initiatory esoterism, the political nature of Maimonides's reticence.

For Strauss, Maimonides is not a depository of a *philosophia perennis*, nor the representative of an initiatory-esoteric tradition: his teachings founded on the use of speculative premises, and so rational, are secret only because the aims and needs of philosophy do not coincide with those of the political society, just as the search for truth does not coincide with the search for consensus.

Straussian hermeneutics is neither a theory of hermetic experience nor a universal theory of the hermeneutic experience, but rather a rational research method, concrete and flexible.[10] Strauss's hermeneutic conception is closely linked to a rational, antitraditional, and anticonformist conception of philosophical activity, in which reticence is seen as a direct consequence of the need to interpret philosophical activity as education. Also present in societies in which there is no censorship, reticent literature does not depend only on the presence of forms of political and religious persecution. Without doubt the influence of persecution on literature pushes heterodox authors towards the elaboration of a particular literary technique that uses silences, repetitions, contradictions, and ambiguous words in order to communicate the truth on fundamental issues exclusively between the lines. From this perspective, reticent writing—used in different forms by Plato and Xenophon, Averroes and Avicenna, Maimonides and Spinoza, Machiavelli and Hobbes—is a necessary form of defence of philosophy (and of philosophers). For this reason reticent writing can be identified with a certain facility in all those authors who have found themselves in situations of political or religious persecution. However, the ambit of Straussian hermeneutics extends well beyond an analysis of historical contingencies, applying in principle to all authors in the past who accepted the distinction between esoteric and exoteric thought, leaving various aspects of their teaching implicit. By limiting themselves to providing only a few hints towards the theoretical truth within a discourse in other ways coherent, the philosophers manage to remedy the essentially limited nature of writing: the art of reticent writing provides a method for saying different things to different readers. The attention of the interpreter must therefore focus on the obscurities, contradictions, repetitions, omissions, errors, and silences in the text with the aim of bringing an indirect light to the true designs of the author, since the presence of these irregularities, thematic and formal, consists in the formulation of unconventional opinions. A reticent book contains two teachings: one edifying and found on the surface and one philosophical and appearing exclusively between the lines. The reader of a reticent text can thus follow a path that leads from common opinions to theoretical concepts and truths, but can also remain inseparably linked to the world of the imagination. Exterior conformity with the opinions of the community in which one lives is an indispensable prerequisite for a philosopher, and the process of substitution of opinions with truth can be conducted only gradually and in an esoteric manner.

In direct contradiction with the historicist tradition, which claims the priority of the historical-social dimension above that of the individual, Straussian interpretation aims to grasp what might be defined as oral teachings—in other words, private teachings—found hidden within publicly visible, written teachings. No historian can understand the secret thoughts of an individual personality starting from the given historical context: on this basis it is possible to reconstruct only the most obvious facts and opinions that represent the common denominators of the era. The mere existence of reticent literature therefore implies the abandonment of all prospects of historical reconstruction determined and oriented in idealistic, historicist, or sociological terms. No Hegelian and post-Hegelian Zeitgeist has the right of citizenship in the study of classical texts: modern historic knowledge arose in coincidence with the interruption of the esoteric tradition. For this reason, in his reading of the *Guide*, Strauss considers the nuances in their minimum details: no word is superfluous or accidental in a work of great literary and conceptual perfection. In this sense Strauss strives to define down to the smallest details a procedure for legitimate reading between the lines, trying to circumscribe the characteristics and the functions of the methodologies, the analytic instruments, and the rhetorical figures implied in his interpretation of the *Guide*, arriving at the definition of a genuine interpretive technique that takes into consideration—alongside the content—the formal structure, because in works of literary perfection the content depends on the style. Philosophy is a discourse of a particular genre that requires the fine tuning of a procedure of gradual introduction to the philosophical discourse itself, concretely expressed in the art of reticent writing. In the Straussian interpretation, the gradual but necessary introduction to philosophy is defined as "liberal education"; that is, education for the perfection of people, because philosophy, as a search for wisdom, is simultaneously virtue and happiness.

Persecution and conformism are not capable of impeding the existence and public expression of independent thought. In the Straussian interpretation, the influence of persecution on literature pushes heterodox authors towards the elaboration of a particular literary technique, using silences, repetitions, and contradictions to communicate the truth on fundamental issues exclusively between the lines. But to sustain the correctness of historical research that emerges from this hermeneutic conception, Strauss writes explicitly of a legitimate use and an illegitimate use of reading between the lines.

> The historian will merely, and rightly, demand that in spite of all changes which have occurred or which will occur in the intellectual climate, the tradition of historical exactness shall be continued. Accordingly, he will not accept an arbitrary standard of exactness which might exclude a priori the most important facts of the past from human knowledge, but will adapt the rules of certainty which guide his research to the nature of his subject. He will then follow such rules as these: reading between the lines is strictly prohibited in all cases where it would be less exact than not doing so. Only such reading between the lines as starts from an exact consideration of the explicit statements of the author is legitimate. The context in which a statement occurs, and the literary character of the whole work as well as its plan, must be perfectly understood before an interpretation of the statement can reasonably claim to be adequate or even correct. One is not entitled to delete a

> passage, nor to emend its text, before one has fully considered all reasonable possibilities of understanding the passage as it stands—one of these possibilities being that the passage may be ironic. If a master of the art of writing commits such blunders as would shame an intelligent high school boy, it is reasonable to assume that they are intentional, especially if the author discusses, however incidentally, the possibility of intentional blunders in writing. The views of the author of a drama or dialogue must not, without previous proof, be identified with the views expressed by one or more of his characters, or with those agreed upon by all his characters or by his attractive characters. The real opinion of an author is not necessarily identical with that which he expresses in the largest number of passages.[11]

Strauss's hermeneutic vindication, explicitly at odds with modern historical and historiographic trends, concentrates on detailed textual analysis with the aim of making the classical texts—rather than their contemporary interpreters—speak. The attention of the interpreter must contemplate the obscurities, contradictions, repetitions, omissions, errors, and silences of the text with the aim of bringing an indirect light on to the true design set out by the author, because the presence of these various irregularities, simultaneously thematic and formal, consists in the simulation of unconventional opinions. The words require an interpretation: the typeface of the text is often a facade intended to hide the truth. Of course, the true meaning of certain terms is not always the literal meaning, also because it is impossible to establish the meaning of a term without considering the context in which it is found. In this sense, whenever an unexpected change, an elementary error, an obvious contradiction, or a marked silence is encountered in texts of the highest level, an explanation must be found through conjectural analysis of these apparent irregularities.

Naturally, reticent writing can be identified with a certain facility in all those authors who have found themselves in contexts of political or religious persecution, but the ambit of reference of Straussian thought goes beyond analysis of historical contingencies, extending in principle to all authors of the past who accepted the distinction between esoteric and exoteric thought, leaving various aspects of their teaching implicit. The problem of reticence is not identifiable *tout court* with the problem of religious or political persecution, and the fundamental political role played by the reticent writing method in favor of philosophical thought is not lost even in the context of an authentically liberal society. Even in societies in which there are no forms of censorship or persecution, reticent literature fulfils the task of responding to the problem of education, one of the central issues for political philosophy. Nevertheless, as regards the relationship between education and reticent writing—also relative to the distinction between two different human types—Strauss notes a great change between the ancients and moderns:

> What attitude people adopt toward freedom of public discussion, depends decisively on what they think about popular education and its limits. Generally speaking, premodern philosophers were more timid in this respect than modern philosophers. After about the middle of the seventeenth century an ever-increasing number of heterodox philosophers who had suffered from persecution published their books not only to communicate their thoughts but also because they desired to contribute to the abolition of persecution as such. They believed that suppression of free inquiry, and of publication of the results of free inquiry, was accidental, an outcome of the faulty construction of the body politic, and that the kingdom of general darkness could be replaced by the republic of universal light. They looked forward to a time when, as a result of the progress of popular education, practically complete freedom of speech would be possible [. . .]. They concealed their views only far enough to protect themselves as well as possible from persecution; had they been more subtle than that, they would have defeated their purpose, which was to enlighten an ever-increasing number of people who were not potential philosophers [. . .]. The attitude of an earlier type of writers was fundamentally different. They believed that the gulf separating "the wise" and "the vulgar" was a basic fact of human nature which could not be influenced by any progress of popular

> education: philosophy, or science, was essentially a privilege of "the few." They were convinced that philosophy as such was suspect to, and hated by, the majority of men. Even if they had had nothing to fear from any particular political quarter, those who started from that assumption would have been driven to the conclusion that public communication of the philosophic or scientific truth was impossible or undesirable, not only for the time being but for all times. They must conceal their opinions from all but philosophers, either by limiting themselves to oral instruction of a carefully selected group of pupils, or by writing about the most important subject by means of "brief indication."[12]

The radical nature of the schism between ancient and modern leads naturally not only to two distinct popular conceptions of education, but also to two distinct conceptions of philosophical activity, basically two distinct conceptions of the relationship between philosophy and political society. This epochal schism, brought into sharp focus by the theme of reticent writing, cannot be characterized from a historical point of view only, as the progressive abandonment of inquisitional practices by the political and religious authorities. It involves the issue of the limits to the freedom of expression in the various stages of communication and public education. Against the contingent imperfections of the "realm of shadows," modern philosophers concentrate their attention on the progress achieved by education and popular instruction, because they consider that philosophy and political society are corresponding. In contrast, in the eyes of the classical Greeks, the aim of philosophers is radically different from that pursued by non-philosophers: independently of any incidental progress of the educational system, "the philosopher and non philosophers cannot share decisions that are sincere."[13] In this sense, the radicalism of philosophical thought is not possible except through the moderation of reticent writing, this art being the form in which philosophy shows itself to the city. In the Straussian interpretation, reticent writing is the sphere in which the problematic relationship between the world of philosophy and the political world is revealed.

The city needs philosophy only in a moderated form: politics is characterized by principles of prudence in relation to tradition, gods, and private and public interests, in relation to which philosophy is, and has to be, indifferent. This means acknowledging and justifying the moderated, nonradical character of the requests that can be directed to the political realm, with the consequence that unconditional philosophical truths cannot be realized within the political field. In this perspective, for Strauss, political conservatism appears to be simply the other side of the medallion of philosophical radicalism.

Political philosophy cannot be conservative, given that it is founded on the knowledge of the superiority of the good and noble above the traditional and old; on the other hand, it is aware that every political society is a particular society, closed to the exterior, founded on a myth which is belief, not knowledge, but is necessary in order to preserve the possibility of a social order. The logical superiority of private life (philosophical) over public life (political) is thus an inverse reflection of the chronological precedence of political life over philosophical life: philosophy is superior to politics, but philosophical activity is impossible without a social life. Theoretical truth is therefore not politically realizable and is also socially dangerous both for politics, because it risks undermining the convictions and beliefs that underlie the system of social cohabitation, and for philosophers, because it leads to widespread social precariousness that gives rise to the phenomenon of persecution.

The solution to this problem is provided by reticent writing, which enables philosophers to say different things to different people. In the Straussian interpretation, reticent writing and political philosophy appear, together and simultaneously, to indicate the problematic relationship between the world of philosophy and the world of politics. 'Political' in this sense does not denote only a specific sector of philosophy, that of political philosophy; 'political' here denotes a fundamental aspect of all philosophy. Political philosophy is the political management of philosophy.

Philosophers of the past normally wrote their texts in the same way that they had encountered in the authors who had preceded them; and so the characteristic model for reticent writing that permits the transmission of philosophical knowledge is *mimesis*. Philosophy is a discourse of a particular genre that requires, in the transition through the various generations of philosophers and the relationship between philosophers and young potential philosophers, the fine-tuning of a gradual process of introduction to the philosophical discourse itself. In the Straussian interpretation the gradual but necessary introduction to philosophy is defined, starting from the example of the classical Greeks, as education in reading and writing particular genres: philosophy is liberal education in the highest sense; it is education for the perfection of people. Liberal education consists in the careful study of the works left to us by the great philosophers, which means acquiring profound awareness of the fact that the great thinkers do not say the same things on the most important issues. Even without being philosophers, we can find that it is possible to love philosophy—in other words follow the dialogue between the great philosophers through the study of their works. However, this dialogue cannot take place without study: all the great philosophers express themselves in monologues, even when they write dialogues. The task of the scholar consists in trying to transform these monologues into dialogues: the scholar lives within an enchanted circle, protected by the work of the philosophers that confronted issues without remaining in the shadow of any form of authority. In this sense the great works reveal their full meaning, as was intended by the authors, only by our meditating on them day and night:

> Those to whom such books are truly addressed are neither the unphilosophical majority nor the perfect philosopher as such, but the young men who might become philosophers: the potential philosophers are to be led step by step from the popular views which are indispensable for all practical and political purposes to the truth which is merely and purely theoretical [. . .]. All books of that kind owe their existence to the love of the mature philosopher for the puppies of his race, by whom he wants to be loved in turn: all exoteric books are "written speeches caused by love" [. . .]. In Plato's *Banquet*, Alcibiades compares Socrates and his speeches to certain sculptures which are very ugly from the outside, but within have most beautiful images of things divine. The works of the great writers of the past are very beautiful even from without. And yet their visible

beauty is sheer ugliness, compared with the beauty of those hidden treasures which disclose themselves only after very long, never easy, but always pleasant work. This always difficult but always pleasant work is, I believe, what the philosophers had in mind when they recommended education. Education, they felt, is the only answer to the always pressing question, to the political question par excellence, of how to reconcile order which is not oppression with freedom which is not license.[14]

NOTES

1. Plutarch, *Quomodo quis suos in virtute sentiat profectus*, 79a.
2. Cf. *RKS* in *GS 1* (English translation in *SCR*); *Philosophie und Gesetz* (Berlin: Schocken Verlag, 1935) in *GS 2* (English translation in *PL*).
3. On the relationships between philosophy and the history of philosophy in Strauss, cf. Thomas L. Pangle and Nathan Tarcov, "Epilogue: Leo Strauss and the History of Political Philosophy," in *HPP*; Rémi Brague, "Athènes, Jérusalem, La Mecque. L'interprétation *musulmane* de la philosophie grecque chez Leo Strauss," in *Revue de Métaphysique et de Morale* 94 (1989): 309–336; Nathan Tarcov, "On a Certain Critique of Straussianism," in *Review of Politics* 53 (1991): 3–18; Carlo Altini, "Beyond Historicism: Collingwood, Strauss, Momigliano," in *Interpretation* 34 (2006): 47–66.
4. *NRH*, 40–42.
5. *WIPP*, 26.
6. OCPH, 575.
7. OCPH, 583–584.
8. OCPH, 585–586.
9. Cf. R.
10. Cf. CCWM.
11. *PAW*, 29–30.
12. *PAW*, 33–35.
13. Cf. *LAM*, 14.
14. *PAW*, 36–37.

Loyalty and Love of Wisdom in Plato's *Republic*

Alessandra Fussi

1. ZETETIC PHILOSOHY

Leo Strauss wrote extensively on classical philosophy. When he compared ancient philosophers to modern thinkers, he almost invariably expressed preference for the former. He did not consider the Greeks in light of the modern academic distinctions between poets, historians, and philosophers: Xenophon, Aristophanes, Thucydides, Herodotus, and Lucretius were for Strauss the source of equally deep philosophical insights.[1] He devoted as much attention to their texts as he did to those written by Plato or Aristotle.

However, it would be fair to say that from the very beginning to the end of his philosophical career Strauss not only loved and studied Plato, but thought along with Plato and in a deeply Platonic way about the problems he identified as fundamental. In order to come to his own way of thinking, Strauss had to turn away from historicism and recover a different possibility for philosophy, one he found exemplified in the Platonic dialogues.[2]

Like Plato, Strauss did not identify philosophy with a system or think it necessary for philosophy to abandon everyday language for technical jargon. Reflection on Platonic writing made him suspicious of the attraction exerted by science over philosophy and aware of the danger of succumbing to the charm of either technicism or poetry: the mathematical side exemplified in philosophical arguments and the poetic side exemplified in the mythic and dramatic aspects of the dialogues symbolized for Strauss two necessary modalities of addressing reality. Dispensing with one and embracing the other would be a constant temptation for philosophical thinking and one to which Plato never succumbed.

Strauss was a rationalist, but precisely because he was wary of all forms of infatuation he considered the modern stress on argument, on method, and on systematic thinking at the expense of ordinary language not as a welcome improvement in rigorous thinking, but rather as a symptom of weakness. The incompleteness and instability of philosophy as love of knowledge, replaced by the jargon of competence, revealed itself as a form of unwarranted anthropocentrism. While for the ancients the focus of inquiry and the highest object of knowledge was the cosmos, according to Strauss's diagnosis most modern thinkers succumbed to a fascination with the human mind, which led them to understand knowledge not as the result of a reaching out towards reality, but rather as a form of production:

> One has only to look at the titles of the most famous books of modern philosophy to see that philosophy is, or tends to become, analysis of the human mind. [. . .]. The underlying idea, which shows itself not in all places clearly but in some places very clearly, is that all truths or all meaning, all order, all beauty, originate in the thinking subject, in human thought, in man. Some famous formulations: "We known only what we make"—Hobbes. "Understanding prescribes nature its laws"—Kant. "I have discovered a spontaneity little known previously of the monads of the thoughts"—Leibniz. To give you a very simple popular example, certain human pursuits which were formerly called imitative arts are now called creative arts. One

> must not forget that even the atheistic, materialistic thinkers of classical antiquity took it for granted that man is subject to something higher than himself, *e.g.* the whole cosmic order, and that man is not the origin of all meaning.[3]

Strauss refused to treat philosophy as an object of study; that is, as a professional field of inquiry; rather, following Plato's and Xenophon's Socrates, he considered it as a way of life, actually as the best way of life and the only one promising a form of happiness not fraught with anxiety and absurd hopes. The happiness of philosophy in the Platonic sense goes together with the courage to face the fragility of human life, the defective nature of politics, and the narrow role of morality.

In Strauss's view (which, as we see, corresponds to one of the central teachings he found expressed in Plato's *Republic*), only the pursuit of knowledge; that is, only the contemplative life, can achieve real virtue. Political virtue or the virtue based on habit and the acquisition of edifying opinions through education is an inferior form of morality, rooted in the impossibility of the practice of philosophy becoming a universally shared experience.

Ultimately philosophy is incapable of providing definite answers to the most fundamental questions. Such answers, however, are made available by religion and politics, and this is the reason that on the one hand politics needs protection from the unsettling power and the tyrannical temptations of philosophy, and, on the other hand, philosophy needs protection from persecution from politics and religion. The open secret of philosophy, the secret that, according to Strauss, was at the core of ancient philosophy and of Platonic philosophy in particular, is scepticism in the original sense of the term:

> Philosophy stands or falls by the possibility of suspense of judgment regarding the most fundamental questions. That is to say, philosophy is as such skeptical: in the original meaning of the term *skepsis* means looking at things, considering things. Philosophy is concerned with understanding reality in all its complexity. Its complexity may preclude demonstrative answers to the fundamental questions: the arguments in favor

> of the various incompatible answers may be inconclusive. This would not make the philosophic enterprise futile: for the philosopher, full understanding of a problem is infinitely more important than any mere answer.[4]

Strauss never published the paper on Revelation from which this quotation is taken, but the identification of philosophy with scepticism and of scepticism with the Socratic way of inquiry is not infrequent in his published works and is certainly central in his interpretation of Plato. Against the idea that philosophy could justify itself only by becoming wisdom, Strauss defended the idea of a zetetic form of philosophy, which could take opinion as its starting point without identifying itself with any particular form of subjective certainty.

The Socratic habit of starting all over again once an argument seemed to have come to a conclusion characterized both Strauss's style of writing and his way of teaching. According to him, philosophy would become dogmatism if it claimed privileged access to ultimate truths gained by solitary intuition. Zetetic inquiry was for him essentially Socratic: presenting potentially contradictory answers to a problem implies an inherently rational and discursive activity.

> Philosophy as such is nothing but genuine awareness of the problems, *i.e.* of the fundamental and comprehensive problems. It is impossible to think about these problems without becoming inclined toward a solution, toward one or the other of the very few typical solutions. Yet as long as there is no wisdom but only quest for wisdom, the evidence of all solutions is necessarily smaller than the evidence of the problems. Therefore the philosopher ceases to be a philosopher at the moment at which his "subjective certainty" of the truth of a solution equals his awareness of the problems, or at the moment at which the "subjective certainty" of a solution becomes stronger than his awareness of the problematic character of that solution. At that moment the sectarian is born. The danger of succumbing to the attraction of solutions is essential to philosophy which, without incurring this danger, would degenerate into playing with the

> problems. But the philosopher does not necessarily succumb to this danger, as is shown by Socrates, who never belonged to a sect and never founded one. And even if the philosophic friends are compelled to be members of a sect or to found one, they are not necessarily members of one and the same sect: *Amicus Plato*.[5]

Knowledge *qua* knowledge of the fundamental problems is a discursive activity both in an objective and in a subjective sense. Objectively, a problem is known as such only once its internal structure is logically analyzed. Subjectively, in order to understand the articulation of a problem, we need to converse with others who defend reasons opposite to ours.

It is only natural to become attached to the solutions we believe to have found, not just because they are answers to questions we deem urgent, but because we identify with the answers. Like fathers with their children, we feel a form of love for the theories we produce which can make us blind to their faults.[6] This is the reason philosophy, for Strauss as for Socrates, was a disputative praxis: our best friends are those who know the difference between loyalty and love of wisdom, and are capable of subordinating the former to the latter.

The tension between loyalty and love of wisdom if properly analyzed is one of the most interesting phenomena of human life. According to Strauss, one cannot penetrate Plato's *Republic* if one does not grasp the psychological, ethical, and political implications of such a tension. The conflict between politics and philosophy can ultimately be understood in this light.

2. METHOD

An authoritative (and still dominant) tradition holds that when Plato stopped writing Socratic dialogues, he also abandoned the idea of the philosophical practice he had portrayed in them. According to this kind of interpretation, the mature Plato became a dogmatic philosopher. In the *Republic* he no longer employed the aporetic form of his earlier dialogues. Instead he presented the theory of ideas and defended his own doctrines on justice, on the soul, and on the good.

Strauss does not think that in his progressive detachment from Socrates, Plato became a dogmatic thinker. He considers it important that Plato never endorsed any theory in his own voice, never spoke in the first person, never gave up the dialogue form. *Qua* author Plato remained hidden behind his characters: the fact that he wrote the dialogues does not authorize us to identify his views with those defended by his supposed spokesmen. Even if we thought that Socrates or the Eleatic Stranger were indeed Plato's spokesmen, we would still have to decide how to interpret Socrates's irony. (Doesn't the irony of a supposed mouthpiece interfere with the message he is supposed to convey?) We would also have to explain why Plato chose different spokesmen at different times. This would require focusing on the relationship between the characters we identify as spokesmen and the topics of the various dialogues in which they appear, thinking about their different communicative strategies, exploring the possibility that they impersonate different conceptions of philosophical practice, etc. The gap between the supposed mouthpiece's utterance on a given matter and Plato's thought on the same matter is not easy to overcome.

Because they are literary works, Plato's dialogues should be analyzed with critical instruments not dissimilar to those scholars employ when interpreting Shakespeare's dramas. Quite provocatively at the beginning of *The City and Man,* Strauss suggests that quoting a passage from Plato's dialogues in order to prove that he held such and such a view is as justified a practice as claiming that for Shakespeare, life is "a tale / Told by an idiot, full of sound and fury, / Signifying nothing," because that is what Macbeth says in a drama written by Shakespeare. In order to avoid this sort of grotesque insensitivity to literary complexity, Strauss invites Plato scholars not to confuse the theories presented in a certain Platonic dialogue with the meaning of the dialogue as a whole.

Since the various theories and arguments are presented by characters who not only converse with each other but are also portrayed as acting in settings that are different from dialogue to dialogue, Strauss claims we ought to pay attention to the dialectical interaction between speeches and deeds. According to him, what the various characters do in the dialogues—their deeds—illuminate, often in ironic form, the theories they choose to defend.[7] For example: Socrates in the *Laches* discusses courage with defeated generals. Once noticed, this contrast calls into question the meaning of the dialogue as a whole.

From a methodological point of view, it is important to observe that Strauss asks us to respond to ancient texts in such a way that we temporarily attribute to the author full mastery over his work. If we note some form of discrepancy in the arguments, or in the relationship between arguments and dramatic aspects, we should think that Plato (or Xenophon, or Aristophanes) intended that particular form of contrast to play a significant role in the work we are analyzing. If we assume that Plato knew what he was doing, we will not set aside as irrelevant what strikes us as a dissonant note. We will not try to explain away the incongruity by appealing to a blind spot in Plato's vision, and we will stay away as much as possible from that form of historical paternalism which makes scholars far too often appeal to historical, social, or political influences on any given ancient author when the real problem is the scholars' failure to understand.

When we are tempted to charge Plato with inconsistency, Strauss suggests that we first ask ourselves why a given passage calls our attention to a certain theme. The hypotheses we may make will be satisfactory only if, after registering several such incongruities, we will see that they form a significant pattern. If we are lucky, we will understand how the theoretical questions under discussion in the dialogue weave together with the dramatic aspects, and the text will begin to speak to us in a new way.

Suppose for example we notice that at the beginning of the *Republic* Socrates is promised a meal and the pleasure of watching a torch race on horseback that excites his curiosity, but in fact until the end of the book he is going to receive no meal and watch no torch race. We may wonder why Plato calls our attention to food, pleasure, and novelty in a dialogue in which asceticism, moderation, and severe conservatism are central. We will not be able to answer this question until we make considerable progress in the dialogue, but we should not be ashamed of our concern with humble details. In Strauss's view, if Plato chose to introduce them, these details can really be relevant. The difficulty is not in the details, but in the questions we ask about them and in the connections we are able to draw. If the connections end up being arbitrary or too thin, it may be because we missed some important link. In that case it is advisable to start all over again.

A serious objection can be raised against this interpretative strategy. Isn't it the case that following Strauss's advice makes us deal with the philosophers we study as if they were god-like figures? Would it not be more reasonable to keep in mind that, being a man, Plato could make mistakes? Why not call mistakes the bad arguments we sometimes find in the dialogues instead of imagining enormously complex works of filigree in which even what appears irrelevant or absurd ends up making sense?

Gadamer raised a similar objection to Strauss in an essay from 1965:

> It is quite clear to me that despite its apparent obviousness, Strauss' statement that if an author contains contradictions that a schoolboy of today could spot immediately, then these are intentional and even meant to be seen through, cannot be applied to the so-called mistakes in argument by Plato's Socrates. [. . .] Does an author really know so exactly and in every sentence what he means? The curious chapter of philosophical self-interpretation—I think, for example, of Kant, Fichte, and Heidegger—seems to speak for itself. If the alternative suggested by Strauss is true—namely that a philosophical author has either an unambiguous meaning or is confused—then there is, I fear, in many controversial points of interpretation only one hermeneutical consequence: we must concede that there is confusion.[8]

In response to this objection, I believe we need to consider that the problem is not our knowledge of Plato's mind (we will never know his thoughts) but our interpretation of what he wrote. Strauss was not suggesting that never in his life did Plato make mistakes, or was beyond historical influences, or never held contradictory views without realizing it.

The issue is not if Plato was a god, but if it would be temporarily useful, while we analyze his work, to treat him as if he were a god; that is, as a perfect writer. We do not know and we will never know if a certain dramatic detail was really intended by Plato to be linked to other details and to the arguments in such a way that it contributed to the perfectly balanced textual architecture we may reconstruct in our minds.

Yet if we believe that Plato, like God, chose to hide himself in the details, our sight will become ten times more acute, our questions more refined, our attitude towards the past less paternalistic, our critical thinking much more developed. By attributing to Plato absolute authority over his text, we liberate ourselves from the habit of taking the text for granted. What is called into question by this methodological move is on one level our arrogance and on another level a sort of modesty verging on cowardice. We tend to give up thinking far too soon when we face a textual problem, disguising our retreat with the mask of historical competence.

Indeed, we could say that the mindset Strauss is trying to counterbalance is the historical attitude, according to which we are all children of our times, and our thoughts are shaped by our traditions. That historical factors play a role in shaping all forms of culture can be considered a platitude. The problem is if appealing to such a paradigm should be our first or, as Strauss would much prefer, only our last resource. The question is whether, when we study Plato, we must use a hermeneutical paradigm that tends to attribute to historical unconscious influences those aspects of the Platonic writings that seem at first sight unjustified.

From a Straussian perspective this sort of approach on the part of a reader could be seen as a denial of Plato's greatness, as an expression of envy. This is approximately the kind of reasoning in which something similar to Nietzschean *ressentiment* expresses itself: I refuse to acknowledge Plato's outstanding qualities (the understanding and the freedom to think about philosophical problems at a level unmatched by most people), and not because I would like to rise to similar heights (in this case I would try to emulate him), but because his gifts are a reproach to me. My failings are his failings. I am subject to all sorts of influences: why should he be free of them?

The envious attitude makes us hide behind the ideology of finitude (our thought is always affected by time, we are fallible creatures, etc.), and avoid a direct confrontation with the philosophical problems. We fail to understand someone without a serious effort to listen. Likewise, it is not useful to decide, when we do not grasp something, that certainly Plato could not grasp it too.

If this diagnosis is correct, then the hermeneutical principle of "treating Plato as a possible authority" is a good medicine. We should ask ourselves whether what we do not understand is a sign of Plato's confusion, the result of the unconscious influence of the times on his thinking, or rather an indication of an issue that we have not yet addressed, a glimmer of light leading us towards a more complex structure, an invitation to search further.

Plato's dialogues become invitations to think along, and our envy transforms itself into emulation. From an Aristotelian point of view, emulation is better than envy: it is not inconceivable that this way of reading may help us become better people.

Strauss wrote a very interesting polemical essay on Collingwood's philosophy of history. One central point in that essay is Collingwood's claim that the Greeks were not aware of history and did not understand the importance of a tradition. Strauss responded to that claim in a way that is not just methodologically interesting, but offers us an important insight into his interpretation of Plato's *Republic*. The central problem is the difference between the ancestral and the good. Let us now turn to this issue.

3. ON THE DIFFERENCE BETWEEN THE ANCESTRAL AND THE GOOD

In his *The Idea of History*, Collingwood claims that one of the chief reasons why the Greeks showed a still immature conception of history is that they lacked "a consciousness of age-long tradition molding the life of one generation after another into a uniform pattern."[9] Strauss responds by quoting the exchange between the old Egyptian priest and Timaeus from Plato's *Timaeus*:

> The Greeks were perfectly conscious of the existence of "age-long traditions molding the life of one generation after another into a uniform pattern." But they believed, or at any rate Plato believed or suggested, that Greek life—in contradistinction especially to Egyptian life—was not dominated by such traditions: "you Greeks are always children . . . you are, all of you, young in soul; for you do not possess in your souls a single ancient opinion transmitted by old tradition nor a single piece of learning that is hoary with age." The Greeks were less dominated by age-long traditions than were other nations because there lived in their midst men who had the habit of questioning such traditions, *i.e.* philosophers. In other words, there was a greater awareness in Greece than elsewhere of the essential difference between the ancestral and the good.[10]

The acute awareness of the difference between the ancestral and the good is, according to Strauss, a distinctive aspect of the Greek tradition and a central theme in Plato's philosophy. It concerns the difference between political life on the one hand, and the philosophical reflection on the foundation of political life on the other hand. It is also a recurrent theme in Strauss's work.

For example, in *Natural Right and History* Strauss maintains that the prephilosophic equivalent of the concept of nature is the concept of custom or way; that is, of the characteristic behavior of any given thing, without a distinction between customs or ways that are always and everywhere the same, and customs or ways which differ from tribe to tribe. Barking and wagging the tail is the way of dogs; menstruation is the way of women, etc.

At one point what was called "our way" emerged from within this perspective. The way of "us" living "here," "the way of life of the independent group to which a man belonged" took center stage. Our custom, our way, was contrasted with the custom and the ways of others, of those who belonged to different groups or to different tribes. Our custom wanted to affirm its rightness in contrast with the custom of others; it tried to affirm itself as preeminent and paradigmatic. Yet what could represent a proof that our way of life was the right way of life?

> Its rightness is guaranteed by its oldness [. . .] But not everything old everywhere is right. "Our" way is the right way because it is both old and "our own" or because it is both "home-bred and prescriptive." Just as "old and one's own" originally was identical with right or good, so "new and strange" originally stood for bad. The notion connecting "old" and "one's own" is "ancestral."[11]

In the devotion to the ancestral one can join love of one's own (the ancestors belong to our family or group), respect for what is old, and a sort of presumption against what is new and alien: neither familiar, nor customary, nor ancient. In the prephilosophic sense of what is right, then, Strauss detects a coming together of what has roots in an ancient and unreachable past and of what can be trusted as good.

Yet one may suspect that not all that is both ours and ancient is also necessarily good. The image of our ancestors must therefore be constructed in such a way as to withstand criticism. Hence the belief that our ancestors were not subject to human failures and did not share our same shortcomings: those who initiated our customary way must have been gods, children of gods, or people raised by gods. This is how the right way, "our way," came to be grounded in divine authority.

According to Strauss, the beginning of philosophy coincides with the calling into question of the identity between the ancestral and the good. He detects important traces of this distinction in the conversational settings of the *Republic* and the *Laws*. One of Strauss's recurrent examples is Socrates's discussion with Cephalus in the first book of the *Republic*:

> In the *Republic* the discussion of natural right starts long after the aged Cephalus, the father, the head of the house, has left to take care of the sacred offerings to the gods: the absence of

> Cephalus, or of what he stands for, is indispensable for the quest for natural right. Or, if you wish, men like Cephalus do not need to know of natural right. Besides, the discussion makes the participants wholly oblivious of a torch race in honor of a goddess which they were supposed to watch—the quest for natural right replaces that torch race.[12]

Strauss makes the same point in *The City and Man*. He stresses even more clearly the symbolic passage from two radically different ways of dealing with a tradition when he discusses the abrupt coming to an end of Socrates's conversation with Cephalus. The old man, who had claimed to be pleased by Socrates's presence and had invited him to visit more often, leaves the scene of the *Republic*, never to come back:

> [Cephalus] stands for what seems to be the most natural authority. He possesses the dignity peculiar to old age and thus presents the order which is based on reverence for the old, the old order as opposed to the present decay. We can easily believe that the old order is superior even to any restoration. Although he is a lover of speeches, Cephalus leaves the conversation about justice when it has barely begun in order to perform an act of piety, and he never returns: his justice is not in need of speeches or reasons. After he has left, Socrates occupies the center. However lofty Cephalus' justice may be, it is animated by the traditional notion of justice, and that notion is radically deficient (366 d–e). The old order is deficient, for it is the origin of the present disorder: Cephalus is the father of Polemarchus. And assuredly, the metic Cephalus is not the proper representative of the old order, of the old Athenian order. The good is not identical with the paternal or ancestral. Piety is replaced by philosophy.[13]

This passage seems to present contradictory views: if Cephalus "stands for what seems to be the most natural authority," and if "we can easily believe that the old order is superior even to any restoration," why does Strauss also state that "the old order is deficient," and that “Cephalus is not the proper representative of the old order, of the old Athenian order”?

Strauss’s writing can be confusing if one fails to notice that it follows the rhythm of the text: it develops in a dialectical movement. Initially Plato introduces Cephalus in such a way that we may take him to be a good representative of the ancestral order. In the course of the conversation, however, several dissonant notes are introduced in the apparent harmony of Cephalus’s character: it is not clear how much of what Cephalus says is determined by his wealth, while his ideas of justice and piety seem to be caused, to a large extent, by fear. At the end of the conversation the pious man goes away, allegedly to perform a sacrifice (but had we not heard earlier that he had joined Socrates when the sacrifice was over?). The defender of the ancient order leaves his inheritance to Polemarchus, who, like Cephalus’s father, is probably going to squander it.

After following with care the entire scene, we realize that Cephalus is not a very good advocate for the ancestral order: justice grounded on fear of the gods cannot justify itself. We also realize that Cephalus’s empty place, the place of piety, is replaced by an inquiry on the nature of justice that from now on will no longer appeal to the authority of the past over the present.

4. PHILOSOPHY AND POLITICS

The exchange between Socrates and Cephalus, in Strauss’s interpretation, represents the passage from the prephilosophical attitude to the philosophical attitude. The identification between what is ancestral and what is good, however, comes back again in Plato’s *Republic* when Socrates introduces the necessity of a noble lie. For Strauss this is a central point in the book, since according to him, Plato shows here his awareness of the fundamental tension between the demands of politics and those of philosophy.

After Socrates and his friends finish discussing the best kind of education that the city should give its warriors, Socrates declares that education is not sufficient. The city’s safety will depend on a certain lie that the founders will have to tell the first rulers. The noble lie appeals to a very distant past, to the ancestral past:

> And I'll attempt to persuade first the rulers and the soldiers, then the rest of the city, that the rearing and education we gave them were like dreams; they only thought they were undergoing all that was happening to them, while, in truth, at the time they were under the earth within, being fashioned and reared themselves, and their arms and other tools being crafted. When the job had been completely finished, the earth, which is their mother, sent them up. And now, as though the land they were in were a mother and nurse, they must plan for and defend it, if anyone attacks, and they must think of the other citizens as brothers and born of the earth.[14]

The goal that the noble lie is apparently designed to achieve is to make the guardians forget that their beliefs and habits are not natural, but are instead the result of education. Forms of education and kinds of governments are subject to change—they belong to the sphere of *nomos*—while what is by nature always follows the same path, and it would be foolish to try to alter it.

This point is very clear in Strauss's comment in *The City and Man*:

> The first part is meant to make the citizens forget the truth about their education or the true character of their becoming citizens out of mere human beings or out of what one may call natural human beings. It surely is meant to blur the distinction between nature and art and between nature and convention.[15]

The citizens (the rulers and the warriors) have to forget that their beliefs had been shaped from childhood by the poets, whose tales were formed according to the models prescribed by the founders of the city in speech (*Resp.* 378e–379a).

The noble lie confers ancestral prestige on the political structure that Socrates and his friends have been building in words. The new polity must appear ancient: this can be achieved by erasing the historical memory and replacing it with ungrounded beliefs; that is, by blurring the distinction between what one sees with one's own eyes and what one believes as a result of hearsay. The story that the warriors are going to hear is first of all going to confuse experience with myth. They will be told something along these lines: "You were not here, you were not educated by us, fallible human beings; you were in fact in the bosom of the earth, your mother, and a god fashioned your souls as they are."

It should be clear now why Strauss found irritatingly wrong Collingwood's idea that the Greeks lacked "consciousness of age-long tradition molding the life of one generation after another into a uniform pattern." In fact, the problem of a tradition was present to Plato's mind. It was so present that he even tried to imagine how a particular tradition could be artificially generated by substituting myth (the birth of the ancestors from the bosom of the earth) for what people actually saw with their eyes and heard with their ears (the education of the guardians).

In the noble lie we bear witness to one of the first reflections on the genealogy of patriotism. This is what Strauss means when he claims in the essay on Collingwood that there were, among the Greeks, people who had a keen awareness of the difference between the ancestral and the good.

At this point we can also appreciate why Strauss resisted so vigorously the application of Collingwood's paradigm to Plato's dialogues. If we take for granted that an author is shaped by the social, political, and religious conditions of his or her time, we will tend to consider wrong a position that attributes to philosophy the capacity to transcend its time. We will not be alert to such a perspective and therefore able to appreciate it when it appears in the dialogues of Plato or in other ancient texts. We will dismiss the portrait of Cephalus as merely dramatic ornamentation. In doing so, we will fail to see that indeed the Greeks had a strong awareness of the power of tradition, and that, furthermore, they believed that being shaped by one's tradition is not an inescapable destiny.

If historical work is devoted only to finding out consciousness of the tradition, we will not be ready to perceive that the ancient philosophers and historians were concerned not just with that, but, more importantly, with reflecting on the ways in which freedom from the tradition might be possible.

Strauss elaborates a very interesting and complex interpretation of the noble lie. Let us concentrate on what he has to say on this first part:

> Even the rational society, the society according to truth and nature, is not possible without a fundamental untruth. That fundamental untruth consists of two parts. Its first part consists in the replacement of the earth as the common mother of all men, and therewith of the fraternity of all men, by a part of the earth, the land, the fatherland, the territory, and the fraternity of only the fellow citizens. The first part of the fundamental untruth consists then in assigning the natural status of the human species to a part of the human species, the citizens of a given city.[16]

The loyalty due to a particular polis, organized by a particular kind of polity, is presented in the noble lie as loyalty to the earth. Accordingly the fraternity of those human beings who also happen to be our fellow citizens replaces universal fraternity; that is, the fraternity we ought to feel with human beings as such. The noble lie invites the citizens to consider other citizens as brothers and asks them to fight for their city as if it were their own mother. A mother, like the earth, is by nature; but the city is not earth. It is "the land, the fatherland, the territory." In other words, it is transformed by nomos, and it is to nomos that ultimately obedience is due, though the noble lie tries to hide any evidence of the real meaning of this demand.

If my city is like my mother, then there is a fundamental difference between my city and other cities, and this difference, an artificial difference, must appear grounded in nature. The metaphor of mother earth ought to imply the kinship of all human beings and hence present a form of morality that aspires to universality. If we are all brothers and sisters, harming other human beings cannot be just (the thesis defended by Socrates with Polemarchus). The noble lie, however, does not invite to universality: rather, it invites the citizens to feel a natural affinity only with other citizens (they have to aim at the good of this particular city, of these particular citizens): local generality replaces universality, loyalty (benefiting friends and harming enemies) replaces justice.[17]

The noble lie reveals to those who want to reflect on it, a fundamental aspect of political life; that is, the ideological nature of the principles that are at the core of what, with a certain dose of anachronism, we could call "patriotism," and allows us to consider that there is a potential conflict between attachment to what is ours (love of our own: the loyalty that in the *Republic* is ascribed to the warriors as their fundamental trait) and the search for what may be universally valid or true (love of truth, which in the *Republic* is the fundamental trait of the philosophers).

The situation of the citizens to whom the noble lie is addressed is similar to that of the prisoners in the myth of the cave. For these prisoners, it is impossible to see that the shadows they trust as natural are in fact the reflection of artifacts (the artificial objects moved by other men on the wall illuminated by the fire).

The cave, according to Strauss's interpretation, is not the allegorical presentation of one particular corrupted city: resorting to the noble lie makes the city built by Socrates and his companions indistinguishable from the worst kind of community from the point of view of the subordination of love of truth to political stability. In the image of the cave there is indeed a place for the noble lie: its function is to generate the belief that the wall, the fire, the men who produced the artifacts, the artifacts themselves, and the men who move the objects in such a way to produce a sequence of shadows do not exist and hence play no role in the shaping of the citizens' attitude towards reality.[18] Paradoxically, the *kallipolis* is itself a cave, and its citizens are cave dwellers. The best place for philosophy in the best possible city is outside its walls, in the Isles of the Blessed.[19]

5. CONCLUSIONS

There is no continuous path from life in the cave to philosophy. Philosophy requires a turning around, a conversion, something similar to the breaking of chains. According to Strauss's interpretation, in the *Republic* we can find two fundamentally different sources of virtue: political virtue and philosophical virtue.[20] Philosophers are virtuous because their souls are in full harmony, and their reason is nourished by insight and truth. All the other citizens, and especially the warriors, are virtuous in a different sense; that is, because they have been imbued with correct moral opinions.[21]

The exoteric message of the *Republic*, according to Strauss, is phrased in the style most appropriate to the warrior class, the *thymoeidetic* class inclined to idealism and loyalty. The warrior class will not find fault in the noble lie because it actually fits with the natural proclivity that spiritedness has towards dividing the world between friends and enemies. Yet insofar as politics turns around this kind of division, philosophy and politics remain at odds with each other.

The superficial message of the *Republic* is that one ought to do what reason commands. According to Strauss's reconstruction, however, the superficial message is modeled on spiritedness. (Hence from a dramatic perspective it is important to notice the fundamental role played by the spirited Glaucon.)[22] Doing what spiritedness commands means misunderstanding the analogy between city and man, and abstracting from some very important things that make human beings what they are. It means treating philosophical *eros* almost as an afterthought.[23]

For Strauss the *Republic* is an aporetic dialogue, one whose focus is not on the realization of absolute justice, but rather on the reasons why absolute justice is ultimately impossible even in the best city.

The book that Strauss dedicated to Plato's *Republic* is itself an exercise in Platonic dialectic. Stylistically it exhibits a peculiar mixture of daring and restraint. Consider, for example, the title: *The City and Man*. The utopian plan of Plato's *Republic* is based on the analogy between the individual man and the city: Socrates initially claims that the city is like a man writ large. However, at one point one term of the analogy is silently replaced. Socrates begins with city and man, but continues with city and soul. The city, which was originally created to respond to the needs of the body, becomes analogous to the soul and its parts. The body and its needs slowly but surely drop out of focus and the *Republic* becomes a big exercise in asceticism.

By calling his book *The City and Man*, Strauss invites his readers to consider that the city and soul analogy of Plato's *Republic* is the result of an abstraction. In the course of the book he argues that Plato was well aware that in the analogy something was missing, and he wanted his readers to ask why Socrates, in this particular discussion, appeared to be so hostile to the body. The part of the soul that is most hostile to the body and its needs is not reason, but spiritedness, which makes us love victory and fame and which, properly educated, produces loyal citizens, courageous warriors, and idealists of all sorts. According to Strauss, in the *Republic* we explore justice mostly from the perspective of spiritedness, and this is the reason that asceticism, aversion to *eros* and its excesses, and a strong accent on the value of salutary habits come to be central in this work (as opposed to the *Symposium*, which, according to Strauss, is complementary to the *Republic* in giving voice to *eros* in all its forms).

As I mentioned earlier, Strauss is keen on finding in the details the most interesting revelations. One such detail is the myth of Er, where Socrates reveals that virtue derived from habit is not at all reliable:

> He said that when the spokesman had said this the man who had drawn the first lot came forward and immediately chose the greatest tyranny, and, due to folly and gluttony, chose without having considered everything adequately; and it escaped his notice that eating his own children and other evils were fated to be a part of that life. When he considered it at his leisure, he beat his breast and lamented the choice, not abiding by the spokesman's forewarning. For he didn't blame himself for the evils but chance, demons, and anything rather than himself. He was one of those who had come from heaven, having lived in an orderly regime in his former life, participating in virtue by habit, without philosophy (*Resp.* 619b–d).

Living in the best political regime and absorbing its values through habit is no guarantee against a fascination with the worst form of tyranny. Strauss referred to this passage on several occasions, and we know that his positions on ancient tyranny were not independent of his reflections on Europe's recent history.[24] One cannot help thinking here of a convergence with Arendt's thoughts on the reasons why totalitarian regimes exercise a fascination that certain types of morality are not capable of withstanding.[25]

NOTES

1. OCPH, 581–582: "In attempting to answer the question regarding Herodotus' intention, one must not even assume that Herodotus was a *historian*. For in making this assumption one is likely to imply that he was not a *philosopher* and thus to exclude without examination the possibility that Herodotus' intention cannot be understood without a complete revision of our *categories*."
2. See LIGPP, 115–138. This conference is a striking example of an anticipated intellectual autobiography. Strauss explains why Heidegger opened up for him a new way to read the Greeks and why historicism, taken to its extreme consequences, led Strauss to the interpretation of philosophy as a quest for transcendent truth. Heidegger made him understand why one had to abandon nineteenth-century interpretative positions in order to understand the Greeks. The Greeks, in turn, allowed Strauss to gain freedom from Heidegger's own influence. (On the difference between the *refutation of* historicism and the *liberation from* historicism, see LIGPP, 132–133.)
3. PR, 31–32.
4. RR, 147–148.
5. *OT*, 216. "Amicus Plato" is the beginning of a Latin phrase referring to Aristotle, *Nic. Eth.* 1096a16–17: "Amicus Plato sed magis amica veritas": "Friend of Plato, but a greater friend of the truth."
6. Cf. Plato, *Resp.* 330c3–6; Aristotle, *Nic. Eth.* 1167b30–1168a8; 1168a21; 1161b17–33.
7. In *The City and Man* Strauss spells out several ways in which the dialectic between deeds and speeches plays a role in Plato's dialogues. For a discussion of five specific forms of this kind of dialectic in connection with the difference between Socratic irony and

Platonic irony, see Alessandra Fussi, *La città nell'anima. Strauss lettore di Platone e Senofonte* (Pisa: ETS, 2012), 84–114.

8. Hans-Georg Gadamer, "Hermeneutics and Historicism" (1965), in *Truth and Method2*, trans. Joel Weinsheimer and D.G. Marshall (London: *Sheed & Ward, 1989),* 506–544 (535–536).
9. R.G. Collingwood, *The Idea of History*, rev. ed. (Oxford: Oxford University Press, 1993), 22; cf. 26, 34.
10. OCPH, 570.
11. *NRH*, 82.
12. *NRH*, 84–85.
13. *CM*, 65.
14. I quote Plato's *Republic* from *The Republic of Plato*, ed. A. Bloom, (New York: Basic Books, 1991). Here, *Resp.* 414d.
15. *CM*, 102.
16. PS, 158. The same point is made in *CM*, 102: "It demands that the citizens regard themselves as children of one and the same mother and nurse, the earth, and hence as brothers, but in such a way that the earth is to be identified with a part of the earth, with the particular land or territory belonging to the particular city in question: the fraternity of all human beings is to be replaced by the fraternity of all fellow citizens."
17. Strauss makes this point in the fourth lecture on Socrates:

> The first reason why the noble delusion is required is the tension between the impossibility of a universal political society on the one hand—universal is meant here literally, embracing all human beings—and the essential defect of the particular or closed political society on the other. The particular or closed political society conflicts with the natural fraternity of all men. Political society in one way or another draws an arbitrary line between man and man. Political society is essentially exclusive or harsh. The discussion of justice in the first book of the *Republic* may be said to culminate in the suggestion that the just man does not do any harm to anyone. Pursuing this line of thought, we arrive at the conclusion that justice is universal beneficence. But this

> whole line of thought is dropped silently, yet not unnoticeably, in Socrates' strong speech on behalf of justice. The guardians of the just city are compared to dogs who are gentle to their acquaintances, or friends, and harsh to enemies, or strangers. (PS, 159)

18. Cf. *CM*, 125: "The cave-dwellers, *i.e.* the non-philosophers, see only the shadows of artifacts (514b–515c).That is to say, whatever they perceive they understand in the light of opinions sanctified by the fiat of legislators, regarding the just and noble things, *i.e.* of fabricated or conventional opinions, and they do not know that these their most cherished convictions possess no higher status than that of opinions." See also NIPPP, 354, especially notes 33 and 34. The same line of thought can be found in ET, 281.
19. *Resp.* 519c:

> Isn't it likely, I said, and necessary, as a consequence of what was said before, that those who are without education and experience of truth would never be adequate stewards of a city, nor would those who have been allowed to spend their time in education continuously to the end-the former because they don't have any single goal in life at which they must aim in doing everything they do in private or in public, the latter because they won't be willing to act, believing they have emigrated to a colony on the Isles of the Blessed while they are still alive?

See ET, 281: "The philosopher is the man who has left the cave and who (if he is not compelled to do otherwise) lives outside of the cave, on the island of the blessed." The same point is made in *CM*, 124–125.
20. See *CM*, 27n34; PS, 163.
21. See *Resp.* 430a–b:

> Don't think we devised all that for any other purpose than that—persuaded by us—they should receive the laws from

> us in the finest possible way like a dye, so that their opinion about what's terrible and about everything else would be colorfast because they had gotten the proper nature and rearing, and their dye could not be washed out by those lies so terribly effective at scouring, pleasure-more terribly effective for this than any Chalestrean soda and alkali; and pain, fear, and desire-worse than any other lye. This kind of power and preservation, through everything, of the right and lawful opinion about what is terrible and what not, I call courage; and so I set it down, unless you say something else.

22. Benardete put this point nicely: "Only if one follows patiently Socrates' argument about desire can one see it turn upside down and discover that it is the presentation of desire by the thumoeidetic that has put on the mask of reason." "Strauss on Plato," in Seth Benardete, *The Argument of the Action: Essays on Greek Poetry and Philosophy*, edited and with an introduction by Ronna Burger and Michael Davis (Chicago: University of Chicago Press, 2000), 410.
23. From the dramatic perspective, the so-called three waves are introduced when Socrates, who is about to turn to an analysis of the corrupted cities and souls, is forced to explain what he meant when he claimed that in the *kallipolis* there would be a community of women and children (*Resp*. 449a). In turn, the allegories of the sun, the line, and the cave are presented as an excursus within the last wave (the wave of the philosopher-kings).
24. On the myth of Er, see *CM*, 109; PS, 166; "Restatement on Xenophon's *Hiero*," in *OT*, 182. The relationship between classic and present-day tyranny is explicitly discussed in *On Tyranny*, and it represents its underlying theme.
25. If I had not met Stanley Rosen, I would probably have never studied Plato or Strauss with the same interest and pleasure. Stanley made me love philosophy. May he dwell now in the Isles of the Blessed.

Engaged Citizenship

Jordi R. Sales-Coderch

The figure of Leo Strauss stands as an example of a prolific life of scholarship. At the center of his abundant output is a dedication to clarifying the practice of philosophy throughout the history of humankind and in society today. What went on in Strauss's classes at the University of Chicago in the 1950s and 1960s was simple enough: the philosophical inquiry of a free individual fostered the philosophical inquiry of other free individuals. This becomes clear if we listen to what Strauss's classes meant to people such as Seth Benardete, George Steiner, George Anastaplo, Stanley Rosen, Richard Rorty, and Susan Sontag. The two core aspects that proved so rewarding were the central place in scholarship given to reading texts and a renewed seriousness in linking common-sense understanding, political life as it actually was, and academic language. A soberness of discourse was always to remain paramount. As Josep Monserrat-Molas has pointed out, Strauss's work rests on a dual logic of civic harmony and philosophical disruption. He sought to give future citizens and politicians a discourse that did not renounce responsibility for the common good amid the individual quest for personal good, and he wanted future philosophers to have the tools needed to interrogate the beliefs on which a society is based without destroying the atmosphere in which the city thrives. This is the power of the "and" in *The City and Man* (1964). It has been observed that nothing in the book is not bound up directly with an account of the explicit conjunction and implicit disjunction of that titular "and." As Seth Benardete notes, the etymology of the Latin verb *separo* combines the prefix *se-*, which means "apart," and a verb form of *-paro*, which means not only "equal," but also "pair." Linking and parting go hand in hand. The Socratic name for this procedure is the dialectic method.[1] Thus Strauss's book becomes even more enigmatic because it has a more difficult lesson to grasp. At first glance, though, it looks straightforward. It offers interpretations of Aristotle's *Politics*, the *Republic* of Plato, and Thucydides's *War of the Peloponnesians and the Athenians*. The arbitrary order uses political science, political philosophy, and political history as descriptors of what the Aristotelian, Platonic and Thucydidean texts are doing in their relation to readers. Seth Benardete thinks that the book's "true title" is *Athens and Socrates* and that it is a twin volume of *Socrates and Aristophanes* (1966). But can a singular city and a singular man show universality? And if so, how?

Leo Strauss begins with the statement that he feels compelled to focus attention on the political thought of antiquity because of the crisis of our times, the crisis of the West. He refers to Oswald Spengler's work *The Decline of the West*, published in two volumes in 1918 and 1923, a book that proved more symptomatic than clarifying. Strauss writes of the year 1913 when he turned fourteen on the eve of World War I, the so-called European War, and says that until that moment the West could have "laid down the law for the rest of the world without firing a single shot."[2] Strauss was born in 1899, the same year in which Jacob Klein and Karl Löwith were born, while Gershom Scholem came in 1897, Hans-Georg Gadamer arrived with the new century, Eric Voegelin was born in 1901, and Gerhard Krüger and Alexandre Kojève were both born in 1902. Examining these thinkers, we might see the troubled state of civilization based on what happened in Europe in the years following their births. These scholars' lives were all turned upside down at the same time. They suffered the loss of elements of an overarching synthesis that was, despite its glittering appearance, always extremely fragile: the culture of the German Empire (1870–1918) as a world hegemonic culture.

The sense of decline dawns on Spengler in the wake of an episode that punctuated the colonial struggles against Europe's great powers—the Agadir Crisis in Morocco in July 1911. The arrival of the German gunboat *Panther* sparked confrontation between France and Germany for control of Morocco. In the end, the Germans backed down. This is the singular event that Spengler takes to signal "the end of an era."

The much-later date at which Strauss penned *The City and Man* was 1963, now fifty years ago. It was published in the midst of the Cold War, a name coined by Walter Lippmann in 1947 to characterize the conflict between the "capitalist" West and the "communist" East. The clash per se, though, was not the crisis. Strauss writes that "the West could go down in honor, certain of its purpose."[3] Rather, the crisis was a society's loss of conviction in its own purpose, determination, or project. Crises have timetables and spur much talk, so that one crisis can be readily linked to the next using the same discourse. This happens repeatedly. Crises and the West: 1913, 1947, 1963.

Let us bear in mind that Strauss's analysis is motivated by the state, moment, or situation of a society. In his initial reflections, the term *society* functions as an equivalent for the term *city* in the title of his book. That is, it captures the basic place of residence, orientation, and hierarchy that define the range within which singular individuals can take meaningful action. What compels Strauss to view classical political philosophy as potentially valid is that "a society which was accustomed to understand itself in terms of a universal purpose, cannot lose faith in that purpose without becoming completely bewildered." It would become a confused and perplexed society. When people become confused and perplexed, they lose their equanimity, spirit, head. The modern project, which is focused on society, revolves around ideology. The project becomes contingent and particular. It entails a way of life for a limited number who are of one kind living among others who are of another kind. The bewilderment comes out of the loss of tension that would exist in a society whose aim was to be greater in truth and justice "than the society to which the classics aspired."[4]

The political order, dimension, reality, or level is present before us and it corresponds to something. One way of proceeding is to take account of it, to apprehend it, using common sense; that is, drawing on an understanding apart from the interventions of experts in specialized fields of science. To take account of what is present to us is to climb, so to speak, but while keeping our feet on the ground, not flying off in idiolects. Near the end of his book, Strauss notes: "The quest for that common sense understanding of political things which led us first to Aristotle's *Politics*, leads us eventually to Thucydides' *War of the Peloponnesians and the Athenians*."[5] We understand two things at the extremes: a sustained effort that comes out of a particular situation or state of affairs, and a narrative of the greatest war, which seeks to grasp the natural situation of politics and the origin of political history. In what follows, we try to pay attention to the extremes before and then look at the center.

1. A SUSTAINED EFFORT

Of what does the *polis* consist? Aristotle gives two distinct answers in his *Politics*. In Book I, he says that is composed of the first communities or most rudimentary associations (πρῶται κοινωνίαι, 1552b30). In Book 3, he says the *polis* is its citizens.

Only in Book I does Aristotle address the city, or *polis*, independently of the question of the regime, or *politeia*. He does so because his first task is to establish the dignity of the city and this requires him to show that the city, by nature, differs from the family and from other natural associations. Aristotle's *Politics* could be described as *naturalistic* based on three claims: the polis exists in nature, human beings are political animals, and the polis precedes the individual.[6] That its condition as natural dignifies the political order is an optimistic view of the whole; that is, of the world. Republican interpretations universalize the notion of political nature as a beneficial reality because it implies that everyone, as a matter of course, can flourish or grow through civic life. Various neo-Aristotelians (Elizabeth Anscombe, Alasdair MacIntyre, John Finnis, Joseph Raz, and, in a different sense, Hannah Arendt) and what became known as the philosophy of Phronesis, or practical wisdom, have given a positivist vision of the endowment of humans for political life. They assert "an overconfident wisdom," in the sage words of Franco Volpi, who also remarked that a Gadamerian philosophy of Phronesis is at risk of producing a modest, rather comfortable cultural relativism that would be more or less "conservative."[7]

So then what does nature refer to in Book I of the *Politics*? The first figure of nature that the polis perfects can be seen in the male-female relationship and the male and female's vital need for children and family. The second figure of nature is the relationship between master and slave in supervised work seen as benefit and cooperation. In this relationship, a person is "the instrument" by which the ends of another person are obtained: that is the crux of what Aristotle says about work, slavery, or servitude. Naturally, the polis encompasses and therefore contains all other communities. In her doctoral thesis on Aristotle's political science, Joan Crystal Cordell indicates that the notion of nature employed in the Aristotelian arguments in the *Politics* is myriad and "in some sense contradictory" because nature is at once that which emerges spontaneously and that which derives from "the dianoetic and prohairetic faculty of man."[8] What we do unthinkingly is as natural as what we do upon deliberation. This contradictory nature, however, seems unable to shore up the city because it cannot lend stability. It is not strong enough to do so: "[The Greeks] think that as men and animals beget men and animals, so from good men a good man springs. But this is what nature, though she may intend it, cannot always accomplish" (φύσις βούλεται μὲν τοῦτο ποιεῖν πολλάκις, οὐ μέντοι δύναται, 1255b1–4). This unusual passage brings a number of questions to mind. The first is: how can Aristotle know what nature intends or can accomplish? In political life when it comes time to hold individuals accountable, a distinction is drawn between actors and their secretaries. Since the early modern tradition, the figure of Aristotle appears to us as "nature's secretary." We find this expression, for example, in François de La Mothe Le Vayer, a friend of Cardinal Richelieu: "He [Aristotle] who is rightly called nature's secretary, seeing that nature herself seems to have dictated what he has written of her in his works" (*Vertu des païens* [1642], vol. 2, "Aristote"). The second question is this: so then from this position in which secrets can be known, what is it that we learn? Nothing less than the "powerlessness of nature." The phrase comes from Victor Goldschmidt and his study of Aristotle's theory of slavery: "The powerlessness [of nature] to accomplish that which she proposes."[9]

But what is it that nature intends and cannot accomplish? Maintain as stable through the generations that increase that which the Greek, master or *aristos*, has achieved by means of his political effort. Ensure that because "men and animals beget men and animals, so from good men a good man springs." In his analysis, Strauss speaks of this moment:

> If one ponders over the facts which Aristotle summarizes by saying that our nature is enslaved in many ways, one easily arrives at the conclusion that nature is not a kind mother but a harsh stepmother to man, *i.e.* that the true mother of man is not nature. What is peculiar to modern thought is not this conclusion by itself but the consequent resolve to liberate man from that enslavement by his own sustained effort.[10]

The tenacity of this effort will lead him to depose nature and crown history:

> As a consequence of the modern notion of "growth," the classical distinction between nature and convention, according to which nature is of higher dignity than convention, has been overlaid by the modern distinction between nature and history according to which history (the realm of freedom and of values) is of higher dignity than nature (which lacks purposes and values), not to say, as has been said, that history comprehends nature which is essentially relative to the essentially historical mind.[11]

History, too, has its secretary. Hegel, for instance, translates polis as *Volk* and speaks of a *Volksgeist* (literally "spirit of the people" or "national character"), which is entirely a matter of history.

Strauss's commentary on Aristotle's *Politics* is guided by an assertion that it "contains the original form of political science."[12] Aristotle is "truly the founder of political science: as one discipline, and by no means the most fundamental or the highest discipline, among a number of disciplines."[13] Strauss's analysis unfolds in five stages: city, culture, democracy, nature, and regime. Focusing on the gap between nature and regime, or *politeia*, perhaps we should ask this question: if Aristotle founds a branch of knowledge among other branches of knowledge, who is the recipient of this knowledge? The *spoudaios* who becomes *phrónimos*. Puzzling out this formula, we may find the key not only to a certain appeal or recurrent circling back to the Aristotelian theme of the natural situation of the polis in philosophical tradition, but also to its ongoing fragility.

There are nearly as many translations of the term *spoudaios* as there are translators: *spoudaios* has been interpreted to mean good, virtuous (Pellegrin), wise, mature (Voegelin), decent, diligent (Tovar), magnanimous, responsible, restless, worried, dedicated, ardent, *valeureux* (Aubenque), thoughtful (Sorensen), serious (Sparshott), noble, active, zealous, upright, circumspect, *honnête home* (Tricot), and there are many other translations.

The term *spoudaios* is derived from *spoude* and denotes intensity and zeal, an active and ardent enthusiasm for a cause or person, a successful remedy against frivolity or negligence. The *spoudaios* converts the *telos*, the purpose or goal, into the *skopos*, the target at which he aims.[14] Pierre Aubenque insisted forcefully on understanding prudence as a possibility of governance: the deeds of the *spoudaios* inspire trust from those around him or her and many draw a sense of confidence.[15] Aubenque criticized all those scholars who had identified the *spoudaios* as a more or less fantastical kind of hero, based on the presence of the term in the definition of tragedy.

Engaged citizenship—that is, the perpetual work of city-building—marks out a zone between intensity or energy and the community with respect to setting norms and stringencies, fortifying the city with sober, earnest, and defensive walls. Such walls have exerted an influence in the origin of the city since the story of Remus, the brother of Romulus, who died because of his *ludibrium* (mockery).[16] You cannot leap over a line carved painstakingly in the earth by a city founder, even if he is your brother, or you will pay with your life. There is an ambiguous network of original civic understanding, an axiomatization of *logos* that measures the fervor of confidence and the coolness of reverence in terms of the proximity of the first citizen to the *demos*. In this movement when things are going well, there is a maximization of bonds or connections: "The project of the *spoudaios* is to optimize performance according to the maximal scope of *logos*."[17] If we leap recklessly beyond soberness, we might say that this maximization is self-referential: the *spoudaios* is one who sees what is true in each case, just as if he or she were a rule and measure of them (ὥσπερ κανὼν καὶ μέτρον αὐτῶν ὤν, *Nic. Ethics*, 1113a30).

The license we have taken to speak of a foundational citizenship or primary city-building that is renewed through its 'natural' repetition is confirmed by the fact that the citizen has the regime (*politeia*) as a substratum. In his 1960 lecture on Aristotle's *Politics*, Strauss said of translating *politeia* as "regime" that "[it] is not a wonderful translation, but it is the best." Translating *politeia* as "constitution," by contrast, has the disadvantage of bringing to mind our written constitutions, those documents in which some seek to capture and fix the aims that must be served, bowing to a kind of political fetishism. And using the translation "political system," a solution that satisfies some scholars, has failed to gain common currency. Let us not forget that *Politeia* is the original title of the *Republic* by Plato, which has been known since the time of Cicero by its Latin equivalent: *res publica*. Perhaps leaving aside the infelicitous "regime," the best approach is to let *politeia/republica* stand as far as possible as an *x* that makes us think a little rather than as a reality that can be pinned down in quiet reflection or heedless folly.

In the dialectic between patriots and partisans, the Aristotelian position is unable to come down on one side or the other. Rather, Aristotle exalts the standing of the "party of excellence," the meritocracy. Strauss focuses on the way Aristotle shifts the democrats' claim that when there is no democracy there is no city. For the partisan of any kind of regime, the city has no greater existence than when it possesses the form of regime to which he or she is a partisan. "There are other people, the moderate and sober people," Strauss writes, "who reject this extreme view and therefore say that the change of regime is a surface event which does not affect the being of the city at all."[18] Strauss is teaching us to look at the density of political life, the politeia as a way of life that is the source of laws and bestows citizenship. This kind of people, Strauss goes on, will tell you that however much the citizens depend on the regime, the good citizens are people who serve their city well regardless of its regime. We call these people "patriots." They will label partisans as "renegades." Xenophon gave one of these latter the nickname "buskin," after the high boot worn in Athenian tragedy, because the boot can be worn equally well on both feet (*Hellenica*, 2.3.30–31).

The merits of a person are the merits of the city—the result of an extraordinary interplay of seeking, education, the defense of customs or regimes, the way of life, patriotism and partisanship, the dealings of traitors or renegades, the tug of fealty and legitimacy. The Aristotelian *aporia* is often dialogical in the Socratic style. There are dialogues in the city between the partisans of the few who become patriots when they lose and the partisans of the many who become nothing when they lose and therefore become even more partisan. These are dialogues between the rich and poor that enable Aristotle to resolve with lucidity the Athenian duality between oligarchy and democracy—a debate about who governs best, who should have authority over a culture, who should command a society, who makes humans thrive better in the polis, in a society, in a culture; and who should take responsibility for the way of life of the people (*demos*) as their ruler (*arkhé*). If this list of equivalences strikes us as peculiar, and it is, perhaps this is because we have progressed from the reception of "common sense" understanding to the *aporia* of a political philosophy. *Athens and Socrates.*

2. A NARRATIVE OF THE GREATEST WAR

Thucydides's first explicit judgment is that the war between the Peloponnesians and the Athenians was greater than all previous wars. This makes him a teacher showing a truth: the weakness of the ancients. In his account, Thucydides describes the road that leads from ancient weakness to the current strength of the two antagonists, Athens and Sparta. Because of the poor soil of Athens, which was therefore not desired by others, Athenians were left in peace, growing to "some greatness" long before Sparta developed. This enabled the Athenians to relax the ancient, barbaric style of life and develop "rather luxurious practices." Yet the Spartans were the first to introduce a style of life that is peculiarly Greek, a style of equality and republican simplicity, "a mean between barbaric penury and barbaric pomp."[19] We have a gradation of styles of life in the barbaric duality of the Greeks: between the Spartan way and Athenian luxury. Sparta's power is a stable power. The Spartans are at once moderate and prosperous. The superiority of Sparta in republican virtue, political stability, and moderation is the flipside of its inferiority in imperial grandeur and splendor. Thucydides's final judgment on the two styles of life is that the Athenians were militarily superior because they were quick and enterprising, while the Spartans were slow and disinclined to boldness (Thucydides, 8.96.5). Thucydides's favorable judgment on Sparta rests on "the goodness of moderation, justice and piety."[20] The question that Thucydides's writing poses to the reader is what happens to the greatest, and his response is twofold: they are brilliant and they do not last.

On the other side of the Atlantic and at a much later date, we see this borne out. The US state of Tennessee was founded in 1795. In 1895, to celebrate its centennial, the state decided to hold an international exposition in Nashville, the state capital, and the showpiece was to be an exact replica of the Parthenon. As in so many cases, there was a desire to have the attraction remain standing once the exposition had ended, and so it did. Many decades later, the sculptor Alan LeQuire, a native son of Nashville, was given the commission to reproduce the statue that presided over the original Parthenon. It took him nearly eight years to complete, and the finished statue was eventually unveiled on 20 May 1990.[21] To this story, an initial observation along Straussian lines might read: "It is not Thucydides' fault if his readers are more impressed by the brilliant than by the unobtrusive."[22]

Does Thucydides's work lie at the heart of this transatlantic fascination with the Athens that was brilliant? In my view, it does. Strauss held that we see in Thucydides's text the origins of political history, political history *in statu nascendi*, still clearly bound up with its process of creation. Thucydides is concerned with war above all else and, more broadly speaking, with foreign affairs. As for "the good order in the city, [Thucydides] leaves it to the moderate citizens."[23] There is a political history of wars not because there are wars but because there are wars and treaties, wars that cause treaties to be broken. The origin of political history is bound up with broken pacts. Strauss shows very well that the problem of "the greatest war" is the appeal of Athens, a tragic appeal. He reflects on the invitation of Pericles, a great partisan of trade and seafaring, calling upon all Athenians to become lovers (*erastai*) of their city (2.43.1): "It was the community of lovers of their city who desired to adorn their beloved with the jewel Sicily."[24] The *eros* of the Athenians for Sicily entailed forgetting everything private in favor of the city. Or, as Alcibiades puts it, only glory after death brings about the perfect harmony between the private and the public (6.16). Yet Alcibiades does not meet with a glorious death. The key to reestablishing Athens after Sicily is connected to Alcibiades's return from Sparta to Athens. Alcibiades, the impious, restores moderation to Athens. Alcibiades's life is truly extraordinary; the biography by Jacqueline de Romilly succeeds in capturing it in full measure.[25]

Moderation, political understanding, or political science cannot begin by looking at the city as the cave. The first step must be to view the city as a world, to see people who are immersed in political life in "the greatest war." As Strauss writes near the end of *The City and Man*, "the present war is always the greatest war."[26] The time for glory ends. The art of playing for more time puts us outside political history. This playing for more time is a feminine art of Plato's Diotima, teacher of Socrates, who held off the plague for ten years through improved hygiene, and it is true of Homer's Penelope, who unpicks her day's weaving each night.[27] Hygiene and night are figures of trickery and deception deployed to buy time against inevitable calamity.

Competing with Homer is far from easy. War does so by growing ever greater than the Trojan War. Plato does compete with Homer, as does Thucydides. We have Homer, Plato, and Thucydides. We have Athens and we have Dublin on 16 June 1904—Bloomsday. Nor is competing with Thucydides and Lucretius simple. We have Athens and then Oran in 1945. Sometimes new writing makes an effort that *drives growth*.[28] This is a striving better directed at sustained effort within the natural situation in which engaged citizenship must operate, than at fascinations captured in the liveliest political histories.

NOTES

1. Seth Benardete, "Leo Strauss' *The City and Man*," in *Political Science Reviewer*, 8 (1978): 1–20.
2. *CM*, 2.
3. *CM*, 3.
4. *CM*, 3.
5. *CM*, 240. Consult 9 September 2015.
6. For a standard treatment of these claims, see Fred D. Miller, Jr., *Nature, Justice, and Rights in Aristotle's Politics* (Oxford: Oxford University Press, 1995), ch. 2.
7. Franco Volpi, "Réhabilitation de la philosophie pratique et néo-aristotélisme," in *Aristote Politique: Études sur la Politique d'Aristote*, eds. Antoinette Tordesillas and Pierre Aubenque (Paris: Presses Universitaires de France, 1993).
8. Joan Crystal Cordell, "La science politique d'Aristote: L'architecture de l'action," (doctoral thesis supervised by Pierre Manent, University of Toronto, 2009).
9. Victor Goldschmidt, "La théorie aristotélicienne de l'esclavage et sa méthode," in *Zetesis* (Antwerp: De Nederlandsche Boekhandel, 1973).
10. *CM*, 42.
11. *CM*, 16.
12. *CM*, 12.
13. *CM*, 21.
14. Francis Sparshott, *Taking Life Seriously: A Study of the Argument of the Nichomachean Ethics* (Toronto: University of Toronto Press, 1994), 52.
15. Pierre Aubenque, *La prudence chez Aristote* (Paris: Presses Universitaires de France, 1963).
16. "Vulgatior fama est ludibrio fratris Remum novos transiluisse muros; inde ab irato Romulo, cum verbis quoque increpitans

adiecisset, *Sic deinde, quicumque alius transilict moenia mea,*" (Livy, 1.7.2). Strauss cited the story in his seminar on Aristotle's *Politics* in 1967, specifically drawing on Machiavelli's use of the tale. Lecture 2, Aristotle's *Politics*, October 4, 1967, 2.1. (Strauss had given an earlier seminar on Aristotle's *Politics* in 1960.)

17. Sparshott, *Taking Life Seriously*, 135.
18. *CM*, 47.
19. *CM*, 145–146.
20. *CM*, 148.
21. The monument erected in Centennial Park in Nashville, Tennessee, may be viewed online at www.goddess-athena.org/Museum/Temples/Nashville/.
22. *CM*, 151.
23. *CM*, 162.
24. *CM*, 226.
25. Jacqueline de Romilly, *Alcibiade ou les dangers de l'ambition* (Paris: Éditions de Fallois, 1995).
26. *CM*, 240.
27. Josep Monserrat-Molas, "'Una túnica per al poble': un comentari a 'El politic' de Plató," *Convivium* 25 (2012): 5–26.
28. The modernist novel reflects a modernity that differs from the modernity of the transatlantic companies. The textual references are to James Joyce's *Ulysses* and Albert Camus's *The Plague*. For more on the novel as a modern form, see René Girard, *Mensonge romantique et vérité Romanesque* (Paris: Grasset, 1961), published in English as *Deceit, Desire and the Novel. Self and Other in Literary Structure* (Baltimore: Johns Hopkins University Press, 1966). Milan Kundera called Girard's work the best book on the novel that he had ever read.

The City and Stranger

Mauro Farnesi Camellone

Written in the form of a faithful commentary, an entire book of Leo Strauss is dedicated to the *Laws* of Plato—indeed to no other Platonic dialogue does Strauss give so much attention. *The Argument and the Action of Plato's Laws* compasses the full scope of Strauss's thinking on the Athenian philosopher, which focuses on the study of a dialogue that he sees as holding the key to all classical political philosophy: "The character of classical political philosophy appears with the greatest clarity from Plato's *Laws*, which is his political work *par excellence*."[1] Strauss emphasizes the eminently political nature of this dialogue, observing that

> one may even say that it is his only political work, for in it the chief character, the Athenian Stranger, elaborates a code for a city about to be founded, *i.e.* he engages in political activity. [. . .] The *Laws* opens with the word "god"; there is no other Platonic dialogue that opens in this manner. The *Laws* is Plato's most pious work. There is one Platonic dialogue whose last word is "god": the *Apology of Socrates*. In the *Apology of Socrates* Socrates defends himself against the charge of impiety, of not believing in the gods in whom the city believes. In

the *Laws* the Athenian Stranger devises a law against impiety which would have been more favourable to Socrates than the corresponding Athenian law.[2]

1. SOCRATES AND THE ATHENIAN STRANGER

In Strauss's view, the *Laws*[3] represent the only one of Plato's dialogues that is political in the true sense; here, the role usually entrusted to Socrates is taken by an elderly Athenian Stranger.[4] He discusses laws, constitutions, and regimes with two other elders—the Cretan Kleinias and the Spartan Megillos—as they walk together from Knossos to the cave of Zeus. The first point of interest to be explored is undoubtedly the connection between the figure of the Athenian Stranger and that of Socrates. The conversation recounted in the *Laws* takes place in Crete, where the Athenian is a stranger and the characters with whom he speaks, Kleinias and Megillos, have no philosophical knowledge: consequently, he does not have to face the prejudices against philosophers encountered by Socrates in Athens. Interestingly, Socrates generally engages in dialogue with a young audience, whereas the Athenian Stranger converses with two old men. When these are uncomfortable with the criticisms levelled by the Stranger at their institutions, he is able to appeal to the Dorian law of laws,[5] which forbids any questioning of the institutions by the young, but allows the discussion of such matters between older men.[6] Referring to *Crito*, Strauss imagines that Crete would have been an ideal place for Socrates to go, had he chosen to escape his sentence: here he would have been simply a stranger from Athens, and could have benefited from the order established by "good" legislation.[7]

True, Socrates never did actually flee Athens, but this does not seem to provide sufficient reason for his being replaced, in the *Laws*, by the Athenian Stranger. When writing the *Dialogues*, Plato does not adhere slavishly to the life history of his master: take *Menexenus*, for example, where Socrates holds a discourse relating to events that occurred after his death.[8] Accordingly, there must be a different reason why Plato replaces Socrates with an Athenian Stranger in this most political of his dialogues, the only one in which the protagonist proposes an actual code of laws. In his commentary, Strauss stresses that the anonymity of the Athenian extends from his name to his very being—that is, his being a philosopher.[9]

In the *Laws*, the word *philosophy* does not appear until book 9, in the context of the discussion regarding punishments for violating the established code. This set of circumstances allows the Stranger to conceal the philosophical foundation of the legislation he proposes. Thus philosophy appears to serve solely as a mechanism for challenging the most widely accepted opinions and is therefore considered to be the potential cause of the most serious crimes of impiety: philosophy is presented as a possible source of wrongdoing, as it can be seen to question the fundamental laws concerning the gods.[10] Since there is no mention of philosophy in the Athenian's specification of what the laws should be, it is evident that he has not made clear the origin and the basis of his recommendations. In reality, he cannot externalize his status as a philosopher and at the same time persuade his elderly companions to accept the proposals he makes.

This concealment of the philosophical origin behind the new legislation cannot be seen as accidental. In effect, the Athenian argues, a true lawmaker must convince the citizens that the origin of the laws he has prepared for the new colony are effectively rooted in antiquity. From this standpoint, *nomoi* would seem comparable to any other *endoxa*, and therefore they cannot be attributed the status of knowledge. By the same token, they do not appear able to withstand the critical probing of philosophical inquiry. Seen in this light, laws have the same shortcomings that Socrates attributes, in *Phaedrus*, to writing.[11]

2. THE POETIC LEGISLATOR

Strauss notices the affinity between *Laws* and *Phaedrus* and explores its strength. The laws proposed by the Athenian Stranger are written laws. The only other dialogue that takes place outside Athens is *Phaedrus*, the main theme of which can be identified with the written word. Given the singular absence of Socrates from the *Laws*, Strauss is led to ask himself whether Plato believes it possible to reduce the hiatus between philosophy and politics by bringing about a gradual shift in the opinions of readers through the written word, such as would persuade them to practice obedience. Such an approach would contrast with the method of directly addressing a political élite, typical of Socrates.[12] With the *Laws*, accordingly, Plato introduces the figure of a poetic legislator: a philosopher, certainly, but capable of persuading citizens to accept his rule through the evocative power of the word.[13] The law in Plato—as seen by Strauss, if considered beyond its association with the traditional foundations of the political community—is elevated to the role of image *(eikon)* of just reason, a point of possible mediation between philosophy and politics.[14]

The theme of persuasion guides the discussion in the seventh book of the *Laws*, in which the dialogue between the three becomes a model of poetic expression that the Athenian suggests ought to be used by the legislator to encourage, rather than enforce, obedience to the laws. Pursuing these possibilities of interpretation, Strauss turns to the reading of the *Laws* proposed by Alfarabi.[15] According to this author, Plato is not persuaded as to the wisdom of openly declaring one's intentions to any reader. To explain the way the Greek philosopher expresses himself in his writings, selecting his readers, Alfarabi makes use of a tale having as its central character a pious ascetic.[16] Pursued by the government of his city, this individual pretends to be a drunken beggar and, sounding a tambourine, approaches the city gates. Halted by the guards, he declares that he is indeed the pious ascetic they are looking for. Imagining themselves to be the butt of a joke, the guards let him through. Strauss considers that the pious ascetic spoke the truth from his lips but lied in his actions. This particular lie allows the ascetic to speak the truth without losing his life. The distinction between words and actions recurs even in the title of Strauss's comment on the *Laws*. In speech—that is to say, dialogue—the Stranger purports to engage with his fellow walkers in actually formulating a code of laws for a colony about to be founded; in reality, however, he is clearly looking to engage with Kleinias and Megillos in a conversation that will last no more than one day.[17]

In the light of all this, Strauss justifies the absence of Socrates from the *Laws* on the grounds of the ban, imposed by his *daimonion*, forbidding involvement in political affairs: he cannot engage in law-making without placing his own life at risk. For Strauss, the theme of persecution emphasizes the insurmountable conflict between philosophy, personified by Socrates, and politics.[18] This tension remains disguised in the *Laws*, precisely because Socrates is absent from the dialogue. The particular dramatic structure of the piece ensures that there is no philosopher to raise the anger of fathers, provoked by challenges tending to undermine the authority of their opinions in the presence of their offspring.

At the end of the dialogue,[19] the Athenian hints that it will be necessary to abolish the Dorian law of laws in order to establish and maintain the new regime. This point emerges with regards to the Nocturnal Council, where the elders will discuss with young people the foundations of the established order, of virtues, and of the arguments for the existence of the gods. With the participation of young people, it is unthinkable that the new legislation will accept the strict constraints of tradition. Rulers of the new regime will have to be philosophically educated, and philosophy necessarily raises questions concerning tradition. At the end of the dialogue, consequently, the discipline of philosophy will emerge in full force, challenging the entire established order.

By inventing the figure of an anonymous Athenian Stranger discussing a possible reform of Dorian law with two elder statesmen, Plato offers the poetic image of a possible cooperation between tradition and rational forms of authority, such as might indeed allow philosophy and politics to coexist. It does not, however, seem possible that such cooperation could effectively be brought about: the true philosopher will always challenge the foundations of the tradition on which the authority of fathers over offspring is based, underscoring the conflict between philosophy and political community still further.[20] At the end of Plato's *Laws*, Megillos declares that the city just founded (in the discourse) will not come into being until the moment when he and Kleinias have compelled the Athenian Stranger to take part in its actual foundation. At the conclusion, accordingly, the *Laws* lead back to the *Republic*: the creation of a successful polis will never be possible unless a philosopher is forced to become ruler. The Athenian will not stay to see his code enacted: like the philosopher-king of Socrates, he would have to be forced to rule. The likelihood of the Dorians taking up this obligation comes to nothing as soon as one realizes that the criticism leveled by the Athenian at their institutions is far deeper and more radical than appears at first sight: in truth, therefore, the agreement between the Athenian Kleinias and Megillos is only superficial.

3. QUID SIT DEUS

In the light of the above, we can now reconsider the *Laws* from the beginning. The dialogue between the Athenian Stranger and his companions starts with an analysis of the Cretan laws. Their ancient and divine origin is discussed,[21]whereupon the general characteristics of the best political order are defined, with a view to their actual application in a new colony. The dialectical approach of the Athenian Stranger is marked by prudence, given that the topic under discussion calls for scrutiny of the traditions underpinning the political communities of the parties in dialogue, hence also respect for the gods, who are guarantors of the laws in question. In the perception of Strauss, the theme of the *Laws* is definable in terms of the theological-political problem; that is to say, concerning the core value of religious belief and observance for the political community.

In Plato, observing the need for a relationship of rule by human beings over human beings is tantamount to considering the human situation as devoid of immediate divine care.[22] Beyond any specific historical determination, this is a relationship that must always carry the problem of justification for the ruling action that guides the political community. In any community, this justification is based on traditions and on specific myths reflected in political and religious practices unrelated to philosophical reflection. To Strauss, this suggests that the view the political community has of itself is prephilosophical, feeling bound by tradition and by the divine as perceived by common sense. Only starting from this basic consideration does philosophy become aware as to the central importance of the demand on the divine in understanding the order of human things.[23] The evaluation of human law is dependent on its origin, which gives it the highest dignity: the answer to the question *quid sit deus* is therefore decisive. Plato sees in the various divinities the guarantors and supporters of that which is just in the different political communities. It is for this reason that Strauss interprets the theological question and the political question jointly, as both come together in the theological-political problem.

We can identify two possible ways for answering the question, *quid sit deus*: one way is associated uniquely with political life, which sees the divine as providing its authoritative framework and is, therefore, definable as prephilosophical. The other way is purely philosophical, posing the question in the search for a critical understanding of the order of human things. From these premises it can be seen that philosophical understanding of the political community must necessarily be preceded by that kind of understanding that is intrinsic to community, by definition. Any philosophical inquiry will necessarily have to take account of the way the community perceives itself, given that the philosopher can operate only from within a community. He or she is bound to show respect for the gods that guarantee political order and for the values recognized by the community. Consequently, philosophical criticism of legislation must have a legal justification, distinct from its rational justification.

The best Dorian law is "the one which forbids the young to criticize any of their institutions but stipulates that all should say with one voice that all their laws are fine since they were given by gods, and should not tolerate dissent on this point; yet one of their old men may make speeches of this sort when speaking to a ruler and men of his own age, provided no one young is present."[24] Accepting this law at the start of the dialogue, the Athenian Stranger ensures his philosophical inquiry will stay within a well-defined legal compass guaranteed to protect him from the charge of impiety, even when directing radical criticism at the main institutions of the communities to which his partners in conversation belong.[25] The Athenian proceeds in the manner of Socrates,

> who prefers to take issue with the poets' stories about gods and heroes rather than with the stories embodied in public worship [. . .]. To the Cretan's remark [. . .] that this demand amounts to a condemnation of the Cretan legislator, the Athenian replies

> that what is at fault is not the laws of Lykourgos and Minos but their accepted interpretation. He appeals as it were from the accepted interpretation of revelation to revelation itself, which discloses its true meaning only to those who never forget that, being divine, it is supremely reasonable.[26]

The Athenian Stranger conducts his analysis on the body of Cretan and Spartan laws with extreme prudence; that is to say, operating within the margins allowed by these same laws. Nonetheless, it is clear that the purpose of the inquiry conducted by the Athenian is that of indicating new laws, designed to make effective improvements to the institutions under scrutiny. Accordingly, the theme of political change is linked closely to that of better political order. Because the theme of change to laws and institutions, per se, seemingly goes against the established political order, the Athenian tackles the subject, in dialogue with the Cretan Kleinias and the Spartan Megillos, by taking the example of his own city. Thus he introduces the question of the Athenian banquets and the associated custom of drinking wine, taking upon himself not the role of the philosopher, but rather that of the Athenian patriot defending the institutions of his polis. And so, once again, the Athenian Stranger disguises the fact of his being a philosopher.

4. THE SOBER RULER OF DRUNKEN PEOPLE

When the Athenian Stranger attacks the Spartan institution of gymnasia, Megillos answers with a criticism of the Athenian symposia:

> He acts the part of a patriotic defender of his city. He thus compels the Athenian to act in the same manner: to come to the defence of his native city [...]. Ordinary people may be content to say that "this is customary with us but you perhaps have a different custom regarding this matter." But one cannot be content with an appeal to the established laws when the established law itself and therewith the badness or goodness of the legislator has become the theme. The Athenian is prepared

> to defend not just wine drinking but drunkenness, *i.e.* to recommend to the Dorians the Athenian institution of symposia, not indeed as Athenian but as sound. This subject came up in a sense by chance, but by dramatic necessity will prove to be the chief subject of the first two Books of the *Laws* [. . .]. The Athenian wishes to make clear, using drunkenness as an example, the correct way of inquiry regarding all institutions [. . .]. It is clearly irrelevant whether a given pursuit is accepted by people who are habitually victorious in war, as irrelevant as whether it is accepted by myriads of nations. What one must consider is whether it is good if used in the right way, in the right circumstances.[27]

The Athenian Stranger sees the drinking of wine at well-ordered banquets as an exercise in public education, which teaches temperance and can have the effect of moderating overconfidence. The master of a symposion

> must be the sober ruler of drunken people. In addition, he must, just as the general, possess knowledge but the knowledge required of him is not described as science (*episteme*) but as good sense (*phronesis*) regarding associations and even as wisdom (*sophia*); he must preserve the available friendship and take care that it is increased by the symposion. Wisdom is so important that if the ruler is wise, it is not necessary that he be old [. . .]. Sobriety is required of every ruler: the symposion is an example illustrating the city; it is therefore more than an institution promoting moderation, one virtue among others.[28]

Kleinias and Megillos, the two elders obedient to their laws and faithful to their respective poleis (who, according to the Dorian law of laws, are the most suitable conversation partners for a discussion on laws), are hampered by a constitutive limit that originates in their piety and in their respect for conventions: they are opposed to any form of change. Their virtue—respect for the law—becomes a limitation from the moment that the problem (as in the case of founding a colony) becomes one of creating new laws representing an improvement on existing laws. From this, it follows that virtue cannot be defined only as obedience to the law.[29] The theme of drinking wine at orderly symposion provides a specific educational function in the dialogue, aimed at inviting citizens to listen and to engage in nonpolitical criticism of political institutions.[30] In effect, a central role is assigned in the *Laws* to the problem of education (*paideia*).[31]

Strauss focuses his attention on establishing what might be the target of the education recommended by the Athenian Stranger. In effect, education can be understood essentially as a call to virtue, although it is not clear whether education is intended to foster virtue in human beings, enjoining a search for the improvement of the individual, or rather, virtue in the citizen. According to Strauss, the reasoning of the Athenian Stranger, with its repetitions and variations, aims to disguise the conflict between the education of the citizen enjoining obedience to the law, and the education of the young, encouraging involvement in philosophical discourse on justice. This conflict seems to manifest itself in a dualism between the perfect individual and the perfect citizen, hence between philosophy and politics.[32] This becomes clear when one considers a fundamental difference existing between the *Republic* and the *Laws*: in the first dialogue, education oriented at moderation teaches the love of beauty, whereas in the second, education oriented at moderation teaches deference. Thus the Athenian Stranger seeks through somewhat articulate discourse to disguise the antinomy between philosophy and politics.

He states that

> education is guidance of the children toward the *logos* which has been declared correct by the law and regarding which the most respectable and oldest members of the community agree on the basis of the experience that it is in truth correct. That is to say, he tries to exclude the very possibility of conflict between law and true *logos* or between the old and the wise. We are at the opposite pole of what he had said in the central statement, namely, that the right reasoning as to what is better or worse is called law when it has become the common decree of the city.[33]

Considered from this standpoint, education would seem to be concerned with philosophy and, at the same time, with politics and religion. This does not confirm an identity, but rather the delineation of three different discourses. They appear to coincide in reflecting the common problem of what should be the just life for humans, but their divergence is seen in the respective conceptions of what is good, and above all, of truth. In Strauss's interpretation of Plato, philosophy, being an inexhaustible search for the truth, is presented as an exercise designed to confute any opinion that seeks to fill the hiatus abiding between philosophical inquiry and the truth: this applies even more so in the case of traditional opinions seen as being of core value and embodying authority for the political community.

This seeming confusion originates in the complex relation between law and logos or "the impossibility of assigning their proper place in a politically viable form to the wise as wise. Accordingly, the best part of the city is and is not identical with the old."[34] These considerations lead back to the theme of the banquets. The men the Athenian has in mind need wine so that they can safeguard education. This act of safeguarding

> requires judicious allowance for variety, for variation of the old-established [. . .]. Such variation or its supervision can be safely entrusted only to old or oldish men, *i.e.* to men habitually averse to innovation. Accordingly, they must be rendered flexible or rejuvenated by wine. Furthermore, they are to tell untrue, if salutary, stories; this requires "nerve," courage, daring, confidence—a state induced by wine. Yet are the old men truly the best part of the city? Wise men would not need wine in order to become able to make reasonable changes; they are flexible because they are wise. Yet they would need wine for the opposite reason: in order to participate fully in the "symphony" of the city, a "symphony" not possible in the medium of wisdom;[35] their mind must lose something—we do not know how much—of its clarity. Wine thus creates harmony between the few wise and the many unwise, the rulers and the ruled, and such harmony is moderation in the highest sense of the word.[36]

The only city Plato sees as actually real—that is, the political community the philosopher finds ever before him—is the "city of pigs."[37] Every political community will always need to satisfy the needs of the body. Considered in relation to the community that structures itself prioritizing these needs, philosophy appears inevitably as a kind of madness that transcends the legal order, inasmuch as it is abstracted from the immediate necessities of human life. On the other hand, since the philosopher is a person—necessarily a member of a community—the acceptance of a political perspective, able to shorten the distance between perfect individual and perfect citizen, between wisdom and obedience to the laws, translates into that more noble exercise of the virtue of moderation. The acceptance of such a perspective must not mean however that the essential difference distinguishing the improvement of the person from that of the city should be forgotten. No one must prefer any other good to the

> virtue of the soul which belongs to a human being and which he possesses owing to some pursuit or habit or possession or desire or opinion or some branches of learning; this end is the same for males and females, for young and old; no one must prefer any other good, not even the city, to this, but must prefer, if not subversion, surely his own exile to being ruled by worse men, *i.e.* to degrading slavery. [. . .] The soul is to be honoured more highly than the city.[38]

The distinction between soul and polis is not the same as the distinction between private sphere and public sphere: the order of human things does not seem properly comprehensible on the basis of a clear separation between the two levels, which remain of constitutive importance for human life per se. The Athenian Stranger takes issue with

> those legislators who think that they should regulate only the public and common life and permit everyone to lead his daily life as he wishes; they do not know that by not subjecting private life to the law, they endanger the citizen's willingness to follow the law in public matters as well: the unregulated private life acts like a cancerous growth.[39]

5. THE TRUTH ABOUT GODS

From the fourth book of the *Laws* onwards, the Athenian Stranger speaks no longer as a mentor to future legislators, but as an advisor to an actual lawmaker *hic et nunc*. In the scenario that emerges, wisdom seems not to provide a sufficiently high credential for political rule: the best political rule is dependent on a proper balance between wisdom and consensus, between coercion and persuasion.[40] Like Socrates in the *Republic*, the Athenian in the *Laws* describes a polis 'in words.' But unlike Glaucon and Adeimantus, Kleinias and Megillos know nothing of philosophy.[41] In the *Republic*, the foundation of the polis is guided from the outset by reason, without interruptions or alternatives of any kind.[42] In the *Laws*, the Stranger suggests that the best condition for the foundation of a polis is the combination of wisdom and tyrannical rule.[43] But, he adds, where the wise are few and the many nonwise are strong, there will of necessity be a need for mediation between the rule of the wise and the acknowledged strength of the many—in other words, the consensus of the strong majority must be sought. Recognizing this basic requirement, Strauss observes that in the *Laws*, unlike in the *Republic*, there is no abstraction from the body.[44] For this reason, in the fifth book of the *Laws*, the regime of the *Republic* is considered possible only for gods and demigods, and not for humans.

The question of legislation is connected closely with that of the type of rule, and the discussion focuses once again on justice:

> The whole question of the end of legislation is identical with the question of what justice is: the question guiding the *Laws* is the same and not the same as the question guiding the *Republic*; it is not the same since the just life in the strict sense is the philosophic life, and the philosophic life is not a suitable subject for a conversation with Kleinias and Megillos.[45]

Unlike the *Republic*, the *Laws* do not directly ask the question "What is justice?" and much less do they seek to demonstrate the superiority of the just life over the unjust; rather, they seek on the practical level to create a political order and provide legislation such as will respond, in the best way possible, to the material problem of community life. This justifies the attention given by Plato to those "venerable and divine" institutions that constitute the most authoritative part of the political structure and regulate marriages and property.[46] Strauss is insistent on the fact that political life cannot be abstracted from the consideration of the human body. This very abstraction was indeed a starting point for the creation of the *Republic,* whereas the *Laws* seem to be placed on a different level from that of the *Republic*. This is a fact that emerges clearly when the Athenian Stranger refers repeatedly to the regime he is delineating, calling it the "second best regime," as distinct from the absolute "best," in which supreme wisdom and political rule coincide. In effect, the Stranger does not refer to the role of philosopher in his discourse: his model appears to be the rule of the gods, represented in the dialogue by the age of Cronos.[47] The best possible regime, the rule of law, is an imitation of divine rule: accordingly, the highest honor is due to the gods.

"Regardless of whether one founds a new city or restores an old one which has become corrupt, no man of sense will attempt to change the establishments regarding the gods: the founder-legislator is not the founder of a religion."[48] Strauss thus sees the theme of change as merging with the theological-political problem. It is at this very crossroads that the question of education is brought back into the discussion. All cities miss the fact that

> the permanence of the laws depends on the permanence, the unchangeability, of children's games and playthings; for only in this way can they learn from the very beginning to esteem what is old and to scorn what is new; the concept of antiquity is the greatest mischief for any city [. . .]. The right kind of piety and the right kind of education support one another.[49]

Thus—as Strauss sees it—Plato emphasizes yet again the difference between two different types of education: the one political, aimed at teaching the young to revere the gods and the institutions of the polis, so that they become good citizens; the other philosophical, aimed at improving the individual as a human being, and thus achieving contentment of the soul. In the *Laws*, then, the question of political order and the theological-political problem are inseparable. With this in mind, particular care must be taken over the penalties imposed in cases of impiety and of atheism.[50]

By creating a balance of rewards and punishments applied in accordance with the will of the gods, good laws aim to ensure that the citizen will love justice and shun injustice. The lawmaker must therefore seek out and demonstrate the truth concerning divine things, precisely because legislation cannot escape the consideration of relations with the divine. Temple robbery or crimes against the gods were the primary targets of penal law. But robberies of this kind are not the only crime against the gods.[51] In particular, citizens can commit *hybris*[52] against the gods by their speech, distinct from actions. Both pious forms and impious forms of action and speech directed at the gods are founded on something that is neither action nor speech, but belief or thought. No one who believes in the existence of the gods—existence as formulated by the law—has ever perpetrated an impious action or pronounced forbidden words; anyone committing one or the other of these misdemeanors does not believe in the existence of the gods; or if a believer, he or she believes the gods do not look after humans; or again, if a believer, he or she believes the gods can easily be led astray and "corrupted" with prayers and offerings. Believing in the existence of the gods and believing the gods to be as the law declares them to be, are two completely different things. The Athenian is therefore bound to discuss that which Adeimantus calls "theology"[53] in the context of penal law, whereas

> Socrates discussed it within the context of pre-philosophic, nay, the most rudimentary education [. . .]. After all, almost the Athenian's whole teaching seems to stand or fall by the belief in gods. Almost his whole teaching is coloured by piety as commonly understood [. . .]. Yet we have also seen that he questions piety [. . .]. But we must add at once that he also is not an indifferentist [. . .]. Being a philosopher, the Athenian is concerned with the truth about gods.[54]

For the good of the political order being established, the various forms of atheism must be confuted rationally.[55] All the same, this confutation needs to be made public by way of a mythical tale which, together with the legislation in force, will give it authority: theology, and in particular the mythical tale associated with theology, becomes the theological-political prelude of legislation. The view of Strauss is that, in the *Laws*, we see the concurrence of obedience to the laws of the polis and veneration of the gods: it seems therefore that the citizen is required simply to exercise the virtues of piety and justice, the latter signifying no more than observance of the laws.

In the discourse of the Athenian Stranger, impiety and anarchy tend to coincide: the superiority of the political-legal order is made visible by the divine character of the legislation, which shows the superiority of the lawmaker both over the poet and over the orator. However, just at the moment when the picture outlined by the stranger seems to have concluded in a harmonization able to make the best political order a reality, one realizes that the crucial problem of the entire dialogue remains unresolved. The aim of good legislation is to instill virtue: but does political life per se serve the same purpose? And what is meant by virtue, given the self-evident difference existing between good citizenship and improvement of the actual individual?[56]

The twelfth book of the *Laws*—where the dialogue turns to the creation of the Nocturnal Council—discusses the complexity of virtue and its foundations: the perspective opened up by this discussion provides yet another illustration of the tension between philosophy and politics. In effect, the members of the Nocturnal Council must not only profess to believe in the gods as named and described by the laws of the community. Given that the council is there to discuss the very foundation of the legislation and the order of the political community, it will also ask itself, presumably, what the divine might be. Philosophy reappears, at the end of the *Laws*, as the theological-political problem predominates: it calls into question the very founding principle of the political community.[57] So can there be an effective communion of intent between philosophy and politics? Can the virtue described by philosophy be identified with political virtue? According to Strauss, these questions—which remain open at the end of the dialogue—illustrate the way in which "Plato brings the regime of the *Laws* around by degrees to the regime of the *Republic*. Having arrived at the end of the *Laws*, we must return to the beginning of the *Republic*";[58] that is to say, where philosophy and politics appear as mutually implacable forces, but also where they are discussed, quite radically, in terms of mutual compatibility.

NOTES

1. *WIPP*, 29.
2. *AAPL*, 1–2. Notable sources on the *Laws*, contemporary with Strauss, include Glenn R. Morrow, *Plato's Creten City. A Historical Interpretation of the Laws* (Princeton: Princeton University Press, 1960).
3. Mark Blitz, "Strauss's Laws," in *Political Science Reviewer*, 20 (1991): 186–222. For a reading of this Platonic dialogue orientated by the commentary of Strauss, reference may be made to Mauro Farnesi Camellone, "La xenia come luogo per la filosofia nelle Leggi di Platone," in *Xenos. Filosofia dello straniero*, (anuario di Paradosso), eds. U. Curi and B. Giacomini (Padua: Il Poligrafo, 2002), 315–330.
4. The question of the stranger is dealt with diversely and complexly throughout the works of Plato. From an overall standpoint, the problem has been addressed by Henri Joly, "Platon et la question des étrangers. Classer, prescrive, analyser," in *La naissance de la raison en Grèce: Actes du Congrès de Nice, mai 1987,* ed. Jean-François Mattéi (Paris: Presses universitaires de France, 1990), 333–357; the same topics are re-examined more widely and thoroughly in Henri Joly, *Études platoniciennes. La question des étrangers* (Paris: Vrin, 1992). A specific study on the theme of *xenia* in the *Laws* is provided by J.-M. Morel, "Le regard étranger sur la cité des Lois," in *Le Temps philosophique* 1 (1995): 95–113.
5. See Plato, *Legg.* 634d–e.
6. See *AAPL*, 10–11.
7. See Leo Strauss, "On Plato's *Apology of Socrates* and *Crito*," in *SPPP*, 38–66.
8. *AAPL*, 2. See Plato, *Menex.* 236a–249d. "Just as Fārābī invented Platonic speeches with ease, so Plato invented Socratic and other stories," (HFRPL, 54).
9. See *AAPL*, 129.

10. See Catherine H. Zuckert, *Postmodern Platos: Nietzsche, Heidegger, Gadamer, Strauss, Derrida* (Chicago: University of Chicago Press, 1996), 161.
11. See Plato, *Phaedrus* 274b–278e.
12. See Zuckert, *Postmodern Platos*, 158.
13. See Zuckert, *Postmodern Platos*, 156.
14. *Eikon* refers in Plato to an image dependent on the dominance of the *nous*, hence an image that shows the superfluity of the idea being expressed, and that "can be seen for what it is": accordingly, it can be seen as an instrument of truth, being good *mimesis*. The concept of *eikon* is not to be confused with that of *eidolon* (associated with the world of the *doxa*); this indicates an image that one supposes to be true, but "cannot be seen for what it is"—that is, an image—and is therefore bad *mimesis* (see Plato, *Resp.* 509d, *Phaedrus* 264a, *Soph.* 235d. On the theme of the image in Plato see Jean-Pierre Vernant, *Myth and Society in Ancient Greece*, trans. Janet Lloyd (New York: Zone Books,1990); see also Eric Voegelin, *Order and History* vol. 3: *Plato and Aristotle*, in *The Collected Works of Eric Voegelin,* vol. 16 (Columbia: University of Missouri Press, 1999).
15. See HFRPL,134–154. See FP, 357–393; "Quelques remarques sur la science politique de Maimonide et de Farabi," in *GS 2*, 125–166; "Eine vermisste Schrift Farabis," in *GS 2*, 167–178; *Philosophie und Gesetz. BeiträgezumVerständnis Maimunis und seiner Vorläufer*, in *GS 2*, 3–123. See also Joel L. Kraemer, "The Medieval Arabic Enlightenment," in *The Cambridge Companion to Leo Strauss*, ed. Steven B. Smith (Cambridge: Cambridge University Press, 2009), 137–170; Georges Tamer, *Islamische Philosophie und die Krise der Moderne. Das Verhältnis von Leo Strauss zu Alfarabi, Avicenna und Averroes* (Leiden: Brill, 2001).
16. See Alfarabius, *Compendium Legum Platonis* (*Talhīs nawāmīs Aflātûn*), ed. F. Gabrieli (London: Warburg Institute, 1952).
17. See *AAPL*, 42, 64.
18. See *WIPP*, 153.
19. See Plato, *Legg.* 960b–961c.
20. See Zuckert, *Postmodern Platos*, 163.
21. See *AAPL*, 3–7.

22. See Plato, *Pol.* 268d–274e, concerning the age of Cronos and the age of Zeus.
23. See *CM*, 241.
24. *AAPL*, 10–11; the law mentioned here is defined as the Dorian law of laws (see Plato, *Legg.* 634d–e).
25. See Mauro Farnesi Camellone, "L'empietà nelle *Leggi*. Una lettura con Leo Strauss," in *L'anima della legge. Studi intorno ai* Nomoi *di Platone*, eds. Milena Bontempi and Giovanni Panno (Milan: Polimetrica, 2012), 165–179.
26. *AAPL*, 6–7.
27. *AAPL*, 12–13 (italics added).
28. *AAPL*, 15.
29. *AAPL*, 17–19.
30. *AAPL*, 20–21.
31. *AAPL*, 17, 22–27. Strauss also points out that education is elevated to a distinctive criterion for political equality, understood not as the indistinct attribution of honors and political offices, but as just recognition based on the merits of individuals according to their learning and their virtue; *AAPL*, 86–87.
32. See Mauro Farnesi Camellone, *Giustizia e storia. Saggio su Leo Strauss* (Milan: FrancoAngeli, 2007).
33. *AAPL*, 26–27.
34. *AAPL*, 33.
35. See Plato, *Crito* 49d1–5.
36. *AAPL*, 33.
37. See Plato, *Resp.* 372d.
38. *AAPL*, 92.
39. *AAPL*, 97.
40. *AAPL*, 46–47, 57–58, 85–87.
41. *AAPL*, 6.
42. *AAPL*, 38.
43. See Plato, *Legg.* 709e–710d. See *AAPL*, 56–57.
44. In the *Laws*, citizens of the new colony are allowed to hold personal belongings (although the wealth of each individual is strictly controlled) and to enter into marriage with specific persons. Family life is not left to its own devices, but subject to public supervision. The

Nocturnal Council is the most important body of the city's government, made up of wise elders who select young men with the end in view of inviting them to attend secret sessions and educating them. From this it emerges that the institutions of the *Laws* are similar to those of the *Republic*, albeit in a more moderate version (see Aristotle, *Pol.* 1265a1).

45. *AAPL*, 59.
46. See Plato, *Legg.* 736c–738a, 771e–785b,
47. See Plato, *Legg.* 713a–714b.
48. *AAPL*, 74.
49. *AAPL*, 103.
50. *AAPL*, 101–102, 118–128, 130–136, 141–154.
51. See Plato, *Legg.* 853d5–6,856b1.
52. *Hybris* signifies a cocktail of arrogance, violence and excess, contrasting with the ideal of harmony and measure suggested by an established order.
53. See Plato, *Resp.* 379a5–6.
54. *AAPL*, 140–141.
55. Strauss repeatedly voices strong doubts as to whether a demonstration of this type is possible, and especially as to whether the demonstration would be possible in the estimation of dialogists other than Kleinias and Megillos. "There can be no more doubt that Socrates worshipped the gods of the city, although it still remains uncertain whether he believed in their existence" (*XS*, 18).
56. *AAPL*, 180–183.
57. *AAPL*, 169–186.
58. *HPP*, 87.

Lessing's Importance for the Philosopher

Till Kinzel

What philosophy is seems to be inseparable from the question of who is a philosopher. The philosopher's enigmatic character becomes paradigmatic for any understanding of philosophy itself. Philosophers come to light not only in the works they write and in the things they say but also in the way they live their lives. Leo Strauss's understanding of the role of the philosopher is tied to his understanding of certain historical models of the philosophic life. A number of thinkers made such an impact on Strauss's thinking that he wrote at length about them: Aristotle, Hobbes, Machiavelli, Maimonides, Plato, Socrates, Spinoza and Xenophon. However, in order to reach a more thorough understanding of what philosophy as a way of life means for Strauss, we would do well to also take a closer look at some thinkers and writers who did not play a particularly prominent role in Strauss's publications. Occasionally, his correspondence, of which much remains to be published, as well as his lectures point to some authors such as Cervantes[1] and Swift,[2] who seem to have played a significant role in the development of Strauss's mature views. Especially in two letters to Karl Löwith, Strauss emphasizes the great importance of both Lessing and Swift, whom he calls the freest minds of the modern era.[3] For a better understanding of Strauss, I sketch and analyze the significance of his confrontation with arguably the most important eighteenth-century German thinker before Kant—namely, Gotthold Ephraim Lessing (1729–1781).

Lessing occupies a pivotal position in coming to terms with what philosophy as a way of life, with its necessary corollary of philosophical exotericism, meant for Leo Strauss. If one considers the astonishing proliferation of studies on Strauss in recent years, it is noteworthy that attention to Lessing in this connection is surprisingly scarce. This may well have to do with a number of factors.

First, Strauss's engagement with Lessing did not lead to any monographical studies on Strauss's part, except for an abandoned essay that was meant to be part of a larger work and that was only posthumously published as "Exoteric Teaching."[4] Scholars have often used this text merely to emphasize the general point Strauss makes about exotericism, not to delve deeper into Strauss's debt to Lessing. Second, a large body of text which bears on Strauss's reading of Lessing (and which cannot be discussed in detail in this paper) is hidden away in his commentaries on Moses Mendelssohn's writings prepared for the *Jubiläumsausgabe*, only recently translated into English by Martin Yaffe. Strauss's interest in Mendelssohn was often regarded as being of merely historical interest, in line with the general prejudice about Mendelssohn as a comparatively insignificant, or even third-rate, thinker.[5] Even though it is true that Strauss ultimately outgrew his philosophical interest in Mendelssohn, it is precisely in contrast to Mendelssohn that his most comprehensive appreciation of Lessing comes to light.[6] Though Strauss's own appreciation of Mendelssohn was clearly qualified—and some of Strauss's judgments in his commentaries have been seriously questioned[7]—Mendelssohn the thinker led Strauss to a deeper consideration of Mendelssohn's most important non-Jewish contemporary, Lessing.

In addition, a comprehensive view of Lessing's extremely complex writings is available only to those who read German, and there is a rather forbidding amount of critical discussions on relevant points in the voluminous literature about Lessing.[8] Although a daunting task, a monographical study of Leo Strauss and Lessing would be well worth undertaking; here I can provide only an attempt to outline some of those issues that could have tempted Strauss, as he wrote in a letter to Alexander Altmann (28 May 1971): "das Zentrum von Lessings Gedanken de Deo et mundo darzustellen" [to present the core of Lessing's thoughts on God and the world].[9] This letter by Strauss to Alexander Altmann, the general editor of the Mendelssohn *Jubiläumsausgabe* and Mendelssohn's biographer, is one of Strauss's rare semi-public references to Lessing. In this letter, Strauss also says that the crucial points are still as clear to him as when he first conceived the plan to write this text, although he did not get around to actually writing it. Thus, a book such as Strauss's on Lessing's thoughts about God and the world still remains to be written.

Strauss's next sentence could serve as the motto for this article: "Das Einzige, was ich tun konnte, war, meine besseren Schüler nachdrücklich auf Lessing hinzuweisen und bei passender Gelegenheit zu sagen, was ich Lessing verdanke." [The only thing that I could do was to emphatically point my better students to Lessing and to say on fitting occasions what I owe to Lessing.] It appears, however, that none of these "better students" ever studied Lessing with the necessary intensity and thoroughness that Strauss's emphasis would suggest. At least none of them seems to have written anything on Lessing that even remotely comes close to recognizing the significance that Lessing had for Strauss's understanding of philosophy.[10] A few Straussian studies about Lessing have to be noted, and some attention has of course been accorded to Lessing in the context of Straussian studies of Moses Mendelssohn. It is rather surprising, however, that even highly relevant studies dealing with the challenge of revelation to political philosophy do not feature any discussion of Lessing.[11] Nor does the *Cambridge Companion to Leo Strauss* contain any significant discussion of Lessing that would point prospective readers of Strauss, especially in the English-speaking countries, in the direction of this most "free spirit." Even the most recent comprehensive monographs on Strauss such as *Leo Strauss and the Problem of Political Philosophy* by Michael Zuckert and Catherine Zuckert either fail to acknowledge the significance of Lessing for Strauss's philosophy or, as in the case of Laurence Lampert's *The*

Enduring Importance of Leo Strauss, give Lessing comparatively short shrift.[12] More's the pity as Lessing does constitute a major if subdued point of reference for Strauss. Strauss described Lessing as "one of the most profound humanists of all times, with an exceedingly rare combination of scholarship, taste and philosophy," before drawing attention for the first time in his writings to the fact that Lessing believed in the distinction between esoteric and exoteric teachings of "all ancient philosophers.[13]

In his work on the theme of persecution and the art of writing—a theme that stresses the social surface of the issue—Strauss made extensive use of his earlier study of Lessing, including material that he had used to write his 1939 essay "Exoteric Teaching." But only in the unpublished essay does he note the work of Gottfried Fittbogen on Lessing as a precursor to his own analysis. In Fittbogen's *Die Religion Lessings*, Strauss notes, "Lessing's exotericism was recognized to a certain extent"; that is, not in the fully developed philosophical sense. However, Strauss did not mention an earlier text by Friedrich Loofs that counts as a seminal analysis of Lessing's position towards Christianity—and that already discusses in detail some of Lessing's considerations of the esoteric-exoteric distinction.[14] As these references are widely known, I can here dispense with a more detailed discussion.

In the course of his analysis of Mendelssohn's writings, Strauss also had to consider in detail one of the most important conflicts or controversies in eighteenth-century Germany—the so-called pantheism or Spinoza controversy between Mendelssohn and Friedrich Heinrich Jacobi.[15] Jacobi's famous report on his dialogue with Lessing introduced his German readers to Lessing's statement that for him, "there is no other philosophy, but the philosophy of Spinoza."[16]

Strauss would regard this conversation with Jacobi, together with the dialogue "Ernst und Falk," as Lessing's dialogues—"which probably come closer to the spirit of the Platonic dialogues and their technique than any other modern work in the German language." Strauss closely links Lessing to Plato in this matter, and particularly to the spirit of Platonic dialogue. Apart from noting the oddity of calling the conversation with Jacobi, as reported by Jacobi, "Lessing's dialogue," it is clear that Strauss attributed to Lessing an art of writing that went hand in hand with his insight into the necessarily esoteric nature of philosophy. Strauss came to understand a crucial fact about Lessing—namely, that he was writing "between the lines," an insight that was a crucial fact about all philosophers who adhered to the "settled principle not to state in [their] publications explicitly, what [they] really thought of the then crucial questions."[17]

Strauss's intimate knowledge of this fertile period of German philosophy goes back to his doctoral dissertation on Jacobi, written under the supervision of Ernst Cassirer.[18] And even though in Strauss's later writings the further development of Jacobi does not feature prominently, it is clear that Strauss knew very well Jacobi's role in those theological and philosophical controversies that can be understood as continuations of the earlier pantheism controversy. Strauss indicates this in a parenthetical reference to the nineteenth-century controversy between Jacobi and Schelling in connection with German idealism in the closing passages of his "Notes on Philosophy and Revelation."[19]

The mere fact that Strauss's public declarations about Lessing—with the significant exception of his commentaries on Moses Mendelssohn's texts for the *Jubiläumsausgabe*—are few and far between may thus explain the scarcity of treatment in the literature on Strauss. It does not, however, justify the woeful neglect of Lessing in Strauss scholarship. Heinrich Meier makes an important reference to Lessing as well as Nietzsche in his preface to *Die Denkbewegung von Leo Strauss*, published in 1996. In connection with the rediscovery of the art of careful reading, he refers to a generation of readers who, in the wake of Strauss, had studied writers like Rousseau, Montesquieu, Montaigne, Bacon, Descartes, Swift, Machiavelli, Maimonides, Cicero, Xenophon, Lucretius, and Plato with a view to esoteric and exoteric levels of presentation. He notes that the range of writers refutes the notion that esotericism is connected to talmudic or kabbalistic sources.[20] And he finally notes that for the new generation of political philosophers that is aware of these things, it may be of only biographical or historical interest to know that Strauss's recovery of exotericism and thus of the true nature of philosophy was initiated through Nietzsche and above all through Lessing.[21] Meier's qualification—the German text says "allenfalls"—that this last point is merely of biographical or historical interest has the deplorable effect of downplaying the philosophical significance of Lessing for Strauss. This impression is based on the stark disjunction of the philosopher's insight from his historical and biographical conditions, a disjunction, however, that is not wholly plausible in the case of a philosopher who explicitly highlighted the nature of philosophy as a way of life. Lessing's importance for Strauss is not merely biographical, because Lessing presents a most challenging model of the philosophical life in the face of the theologico-political dilemma. In fact, Lessing may well provide the eighteenth century's only other genuine representative of the philosophical life next to Rousseau.[22]

That Lessing actually, in Strauss's view, serves as a model for the philosophical life—that he was in fact some sort of Platonist—is indicated by Strauss in his discussion of Lessing's "conversion." Strauss poses a genealogical question: how did Lessing get to know and understand the esoteric-exoteric nature of all ancient philosophers' teachings? Although Strauss knows—and mentions—a wide range of possible sources through which this insight would have been available to Lessing (Leibniz, Descartes, Spinoza), he ventures to suggest that none of these writers was of crucial importance to Lessing in this matter, simply because Lessing was familiar with the sources of this tradition of esoteric-exoteric teachings.[23] Strauss's reference to Lessing's conversion is meant to remind the reader of Plato's suggestions concerning the importance of *periagoge* (a "turnaround") that is the absolute requirement of any philosopher's life. That Strauss notes Lessing's conversion in connection with the autonomous insight or "experience of what philosophy is and what sacrifices it requires" is highly significant, because within the confines of his essay on "Exoteric Teaching" this contrasts decisively with Strauss's depiction of Schleiermacher's hermeneutics, especially with regard to Plato. For whereas Schleiermacher thought that extremely inattentive and extremely attentive readers of Plato were only distinguished by degrees, the Platonic, Lessingian, and Straussian understanding of philosophy "presupposes a real conversion, *i.e.* a total break with the attitude of the beginner."[24] For Strauss, the question of how to understand the importance of Lessing is thus closely linked to the crucial issue of the nature of Plato's philosophy and therefore of Plato's esotericism.[25]

It is further clear that Strauss's confrontation with Lessing, which was also hugely inspiring to him, can be traced more through his private communications in various letters, especially to Karl Löwith, as well as in some autobiographical remarks. At the end of his letter to Löwith on 17 July 1935, Strauss urges him to read Swift—and significantly adds "der war neben Lessing der freieste Geist der neueren Zeit" [he was next to Lessing the freest spirit of the modern age].[26] Linking Swift and Lessing, Strauss enlarges on his meaning in a letter written some years later (15 August 1946), when he calls both Swift and Lessing "die grössten Exponenten der antiken Seite in der querelle" [the greatest representatives of the ancient party in the quarrel] and comments that both of them knew "dass das eigentliche Thema des Streits Antike und Christentum ist" [that the actual theme of the quarrel is Antiquity and Christianity].[27] After noting that *Erziehung des Menschengeschlechts* has to be regarded as a purely exoteric writing, Strauss lists those of Lessing's writings that seem to be of the highest importance for the conclusion he immediately appends: "Diese Männer hatten keinen Zweifel, dass die Antike, d.h. die echte Philosophie, eine *ewige* Möglichkeit ist" [These men had no doubt that antiquity, that is true philosophy, is an *eternal* possibility]. By rhetorically equating "antiquity" with "philosophy," Strauss makes clear that the ancients are not so much of interest because they are ancients but because they are philosophers in the true sense. If this kind of philosophy, however, is explicitly called an "eternal possibility," "antiquity" is not merely the name for a period in history. It is rather a shorthand way of expressing, or referring to, philosophy as a way of life. This also means that both Swift and Lessing were in fact philosophers in Strauss's sense; that is, people who showed what one can learn from the ancients if one is willing to learn—through reading.

Lessing's writings provide important material for the art of reading, as Strauss's list of recommendation to Löwith indicates: he urges Löwith to read the *Antiquarische Briefe*, *Wie die Alten den Tod gebildet*, *Laokoon* (which posits the suffering of Philoctet against the suffering of Jesus), and *Hamburgische Dramaturgie*.[28] This means that a wide range of Lessing's texts can and ought to be studied to gain a clearer understanding of what Strauss was most concerned with.

It is for this reason that the final passages of Strauss's "Notes on Philosophy and Revelation" deserve special emphasis. It is here that Strauss wraps up his discussion of the confrontation of philosophy and revelation in which he tries to bring out the opposing lines of argument as clearly as possible. Strauss raises the stakes at issue by suggesting the seemingly insuperable difficulties for revelation and philosophy in refuting each other. It is here that he closes his lecture by naming and characterizing "that man to whom I owe, so to say, everything I have been able to discern in the labyrinth of that grave question [of revelation and philosophy]."[29] Strauss then goes on to say that he does not refer to the Lessing "of a certain tradition"; that is, a kind of conventional Lessing who has become the object of oratorical celebrations. At this point, Strauss disappoints those listeners who might have thought that they knew who Lessing was. Strauss rejects this notion in favor of what he calls "the true and unknown Lessing." Strauss then stresses the uncompromising (intransigent) nature of Lessing's intellectual attitude in serious matters. Strauss equates the serious matters with theoretical matters—and surely wants to allude here to the theoretical life as that form of life that is identical with philosophy. Strauss follows Lessing in his "innate disgust" with compromises in the serious matter of revelation versus philosophy. In Strauss's view, Lessing opted for philosophy—and then Strauss links Lessing's decision for philosophy to the "whole comparison of the ancients and the moderns" in terms of sight: whereas the moderns may see more, the ancients may be more discerning. This could be interpreted in the following way: since the moderns see more, they may easily lose sight of the most important or significant thing. For in order to know what is "the one thing necessary," discernment seems to be absolutely required. This is all the more true for the philosophers who want to achieve clarity about themselves and the task to which they have subscribed. It is thus no accident that Strauss himself uses the verb "to discern" in connection with what he has learned about the question of revelation and philosophy from Lessing. Lessing comes to sight as the initial and also supreme guide in a labyrinth that can make people's heads spin. Again, the conflict between Lessing and the Hamburg pastor Johan Melchior Goeze concerning the so-called Fragmentenstreit, resulting from Lessing's publication of passages from Herman Samuel Reimarus's radical critique of revelation, may have helped Strauss to develop his own understanding of the philosopher.[30] For in this confrontation, Lessing had famously made the claim that the search for truth was more important for him than the possession of any truth.

In the "Notes on Philosophy and Revelation," Strauss makes a remarkable claim that underscores his Lessingian understanding of philosophy as one's own search rather than possession of the truth by external means (for example, God and his grace). He says, "Whoever is incapable of suspending his judgment in such cases [i.e., the alternative of philosophy or revelation], of *living* in such suspense, whoever fails to know that doubt is a good pillow for a well-constructed head, cannot be a philosopher."[31] It was precisely this kind of attitude that Pastor Goeze criticized extensively. He took issue with Lessing's parable of posing the possibility that God would hold all truth in his right hand and in his left hand the always active striving for truth, although eternally in an erroneous way. Lessing had openly declared that he would choose the left hand's gift, since pure and unadulterated truth would be fit only for God himself. Goeze, in his lengthy discussion of Lessing's sentence, proposes a decision between the always active striving for truth in the right hand of God and the most terrible fate in the left hand of God. Goeze would not hesitate to ask God for his own annihilation rather than for eternal, always erring, striving after truth. If, as Lessing seems to have maintained, pure truth fits only God, then striving after truth without ever attaining it can count, as Goeze indicates, as "the most terrible state in which I can imagine a human soul."[32] In this juxtaposition, the incompatible attitudes towards the very grave issue mentioned by Strauss are foregrounded. Strauss had thought through Lessing's rejection of dogmatism in the most radical fashion, integrating Lessing's words found in a letter to Moses Mendelssohn from 9 January 1771, into the first chapter of *Natural Right and History*, where he ironically notes that dogmatism "is so natural to man that it is not likely to be a preserve of the past." The philosopher's doubt is thus implicitly presented as a non-natural inclination, since most people would follow their inclination "to identify the goal of their thinking with the point at which they have become tired of thinking."[33]

My contention here is that Strauss's indebtedness to Lessing is of more than merely antiquarian relevance. It is also more than a mere context. This needs to be stressed in the face of the current trend in some contributions to Straussian scholarship to apply all kinds of contextualizations to his work.[34] No doubt, some of these are helpful, especially when they provide new knowledge about the networks of relationships within which Strauss developed his distinctive way of philosophizing. However, these contextualizations often try to assimilate Strauss's political philosophy to comparatively marginal contexts and explicitly try not to take Strauss's art of reading seriously. This ultimately turns Strauss into just one more object of historical study. Focusing on Strauss's connection to Lessing, however, leads us to consider the dialectical style of Lessing's *Denkstil*, his style of thinking, as a key to his way of dealing with the most highly charged issues of theology.[35] This, in turn, might also function as a preparation for understanding Strauss's own *Denkstil*, his style of thinking. In Lessing's case, I would argue, his style of thinking is an inextricable part of his understanding of the intellectual life; that is, of that way of life whose concern is above all with thinking and with the search for the truth.

Lessing can therefore be seen as the case of a thinker who fully acknowledges the value and the necessity of polemics in the search for truth. There is no doubt that Strauss himself was a formidable polemicist in his own right. If, as he says, Lessing was at his elbow all the time in a crucial period in his life, it is safe to suggest that Strauss must have imbibed the polemical style of thinking he found in Lessing—a style, however, that is more than a style because it is the function of the overarching desire to achieve clarity about the most important things. It is Lessing's intensity, his deep concern for the theologico-political problem, his willingness to begin new projects and to think in many directions that must have appealed to Strauss on the way to his own kind of intransigence, namely the intransigence of starting again in his attempt to grasp the nature of the philosophical life.

For Strauss, Lessing provided a most fascinating model for the philosophical life under conditions of both censorship and relative freedom. Lessing made ample—but for many—somewhat confusing use of the *libertas philosophandi* at a time in which, according to Strauss, it was fairly easy to "read between the lines." Although Lessing was in certain respects a radical, he was above all an apologist of movement (in thought) as opposed to stagnation and of intellectual flexibility as opposed to reasoning from dogmatic principles. This is indicated by Strauss's juxtaposition of the principles of political and social life on the one hand (*quieta non movere*) and the principles of the theoretical life or philosophy on the other (*quieta movere*) in his lecture notes for "Persecution and the Art of Writing."[36] In politics it can be necessary, and often would seem to be advisable, to let sleeping dogs lie, but the philosopher as such cannot let any sleeping dogs lie. Strauss's study of Lessing contributed decisively to his understanding of a kind of political philosophy that would be able, in principle, to combine both necessities. Lessing is of pivotal significance for understanding the philosopher Strauss, for philosophy comes to sight in Lessing as a way of life and not as an academic job that one holds as any other job. In following Lessing the way he did, Leo Strauss managed to create his very own persona of the philosopher as someone who is concerned with the gravest questions in a playful manner.

NOTES

1. See *GS 3*, 580 (letter to Jacob Klein, 18 August 1939); and LNPAW, 293–294; cf. Thomas L. Pangle, "Preliminary Observations on the Theologico-Political Dimension of Cervantes' *Don Quixote*," in *Natural Right and Political Philosophy: Essays in Honor of Catherine Zuckert and Michael Zuckert*, eds. Ann Ward and Lee Ward (Notre Dame, IN: University of Notre Dame Press, 2013), 382–399. Pangle indicates his debt to Strauss on page 397.
2. Leo Strauss to Gerhard Krüger, 25 December 1935, *GS 3*, 450.
3. Leo Strauss to Karl Löwith, 17 July 1935, *GS 3*, 657.
4. There are three different editions of this important text, the first one by Thomas L. Pangle and the second by Kenneth Hart Green. Most recently, the essay has been carefully re-edited by Hannes Kerber who also edited further material that directly bears on Strauss's abandoned text. See ET, 271–304.

5. Consider Günter Maschke's harshly critical evaluation of Mendelssohn in his afterword "Zum *Leviathan* von Carl Schmitt" to Carl Schmitt, *Der Leviathan in der Staatslehre des Thomas Hobbes. Sinn und Fehlschlag eines politischen Symbols* (Cologne: Hohenheim, 1982), 216. A more positive evaluation can be found in Cord-Friedrich Berghahn, *Moses Mendelssohns Jerusalem: Ein Beitrag zur Geschichte der Menschenrechte und der pluralistischen Gesellschaft in der deutschen Aufklärung* (Tübingen: Niemeyer, 2001), 206–255.
6. See Till Kinzel, "Jüdischer Platonismus, Unsterblichkeit und Moderne: Variationen über Moses Mendelssohn und Leo Strauss," in *Moses Mendelssohn*, eds. Cord-Friedrich Berghahn and Heinz Ludwig Arnold (Munich: Text und Kritik-Sonderband, 2011), 180–193. On the connection between Lessing and the Jewish Enlightenment, see Stephan Braese and Monika Fick, eds. *Lessing und die jüdische Aufklärung*, in *Lessing Yearbook/Jahrbuch* 39 (2010/2011), (Göttingen: Wallstein, 2012), 9–332.
7. See, for example, the harsh criticism levelled against Strauss by the Leibniz scholar Ursula Goldenbaum: "Moses Mendelssohns *Sache Gottes*—eine jüdische *Théodicée*? Eine späte Kritik an Mendelssohns Herausgeber Leo Strauss," in *300 Jahre Essais de théodicée—Rezeption und Transformation*, ed. by Wenchao Li and Wilhem Schmidt-Biggemann (Stuttgart: Franz Steiner, 2013), 115–136.
8. The most recent overview of some important topics in Lessing research available in English is *Lessing and the German Enlightenment*, ed. R. Robertson (Oxford: Voltaire Foundation, 2013).
9. Quoted in Heinrich Meier, "Vorwort des Herausgebers," in *GS 2*, 34.
10. The most comprehensive Straussian bibliography provides evidence for this lack of interest in Lessing through the virtual absence of relevant references. See John A. Murley, *Leo Strauss and His Legacy: A Bibliography* (Lanham, MD: Rowman & Littlefield, 2005).
11. This lacuna is most obvious in the important Straussian investigation of the theologico-political problem by Thomas L. Pangle, *Political Philosophy and the God of Abraham* (Baltimore, MD: Johns Hopkins University Press, 2003).
12. Lampert at least refers to some crucial points of reference, whereas

the Zuckerts, in their most recent book published in 2014 (*Leo Strauss and the Problem of Political Philosophy*), do not even mention Lessing.

13. *PAW*, 28.
14. Friedrich Loofs, "Lessings Stellung zum Christentum," in *Bekanntmachung der Ergebnisse der akademischen Preisverleihung vom Jahre 1909 und der neuen für das Jahr 1910 gestellten Preisaufgaben* (Halle: Buchdruckerei des Waisenhauses, 1910). See also Helmut Thielicke, *Vernunft und Offenbarung: Eine Studie über die Religionsphilosophie Lessings* (Gütersloh: Bertelsmann, 1947), 1; as well as the references to the problem of esotericism and exotericism in the interpretation of Lessing in Arno Schilson, *Lessings Christentum* (Göttingen: Vandenhoeck & Ruprecht, 1980), 7–13. I do not know whether Strauss was aware of Thielicke's analysis of Lessing's exotericism from the point of view of orthodox Lutheran theology.
15. See, with particular reference to Strauss's take on the pantheism controversy, David Janssens, "The Problem of the Enlightenment: Strauss, Jacobi, and the Pantheism Controversy," in *Review of Metaphysics* 56 (March 2003): 605–631, reprinted in *Reorientation*, 171–190.
16. Friedrich Heinrich Jacobi, *Über die Lehre des Spinoza in Briefen an den Herrn Moses Mendelssohn* (Hamburg: Meiner, 2000), 23.
17. LNPAW, 298.
18. See Leo Strauss, *Das Erkenntnisproblem in der philosophischen Lehre Fr. H. Jacobis*, in *GS 2*, 237–297.
19. See NPR, 178. Strauss refers to the so-called theism controversy of 1811/1812. See Gunther Wenz, *Von den göttlichen Dingen und ihrer Offenbarung: zum Streit Jacobis mit Schelling 1811/12* (Munich: Beck, 2011); as well as Georg Essen, "Der Theismusstreit (1811/12): die Kontroverse zwischen Jacobi und Schelling über die *Göttlichen Dinge*," in *Philosophisch-theologische Streitsachen: Pantheismusstreit, Atheismusstreit, Theismusstreit*, eds. G. Essen and C. Danz (Darmstadt: WBG, 2012), 215–257.
20. See Heinrich Meier, *Die Denkbewegung von Leo Strauss: Die Geschichte der Philosophie und die Intention des Philosophen* (Stuttgart-Weimar: Metzler, 1996), 15. This desire to distance his own

understanding of esotericism from mystical varieties may also explain the complete absence of references to the medieval Jewish and Islamic thinkers in his unpublished essay on "Exoteric Teaching." See Hannes Kerber, "Strauss and Schleiermacher on How to Read Plato: An Introduction to *Exoteric Teaching*," in *Reorientation*, 203–204. See as well *PAW*, 111n46, where he expressly notes that "esotericism and mysticism are far from being identical."

21. Meier, *Die Denkbewegung von Leo Strauss*, 15.
22. Cf. Heinrich Meier, *Über das Glück des philosophischen Lebens. Reflexionen über Rousseaus Rêveries* (Munich: Beck, 2011).
23. ET, 285–286.
24. ET, 281.
25. Strauss's view of the esotericism of Plato needs to be distinguished from the other non-Schleiermacherian approach to Plato's esotericism, namely that of the Tübingen school. See for the most recent publication in defense of the Tübingen approach, Hans Krämer, *Gesammelte Aufsätze zu Platon* (Berlin: De Gruyter, 2014). Krämer does not refer to Strauss anywhere in his book. A thorough discussion and comparison of the approaches can be found in Ulrike Weichert, *Von der Geschichte zur Natur: Die Politische Hermeneutik von Leo Strauss* (Berlin: Duncker & Humblot, 2013), 193–205.
26. It should be noted in passing that Strauss's judgment is (consciously so?) in tension with the judgment of Friedrich Nietzsche who singled out Laurence Sterne as the "freieste Schriftsteller aller Zeiten," the freest writer of all times. This would bring the number of free writers to at least three: Swift, Lessing, and Sterne. See *Menschliches, Allzumenschliches.* Zweiter Band (Neue Ausgabe, 1886), ed. Claus-Artur Scheier (Hamburg: Meiner, 2013), 52–54 (sec. 113). Lessing, of course, was very well aware of this writer whom Nietzsche also called "der grosse Meister der Zweideutigkeit" (53). Cf. as well Vivetta Vivarelli, *Nietzsche und die Masken des freien Geistes: Montaigne, Pascal und Sterne* (Würzburg: Königshausen & Neumann, 1998), 132–163. Did Strauss ever study Sterne as he studied Cervantes and Swift?
27. *GS 3*, 661.
28. *GS 3*, 661.

29. NPR, 178. The following discussion is based on the passage quoted here and on page 179.
30. On this topic, see Ernst-Peter Wieckenberg, *Johan Melchior Goeze* (Hamburg: Ellert & Richter, 2007), 186–205.
31. NPR, 171–172.
32. Gotthold Ephraim Lessing, *Werke 1778–1780*, Bd. 9, eds. K. Bohnen and A. Schilson (Frankfurt: Deutscher Klassiker Verlag, 1993), 173–175.
33. See *Briefe von und an Lessing 1770–1776,* Bd. 11/2, ed. Helmuth Kiesel (Frankfurt: Deutscher Klassiker Verlag, 1988), 145; and *NRH*, 22 (Strauss adapts the quotation by changing the personal pronoun).
34. Context is also, of course, highly relevant to the study of Lessing. However, a more thorough examination of the contexts of Lessing's work, including involving his friends and contemporaries such as Johann Joachim Eschenburg or Johann Arnold Ebert, in the final analysis serves to substantiate the claims for Lessing's singular stature. Cf. *Johann Joachim Eschenburg und die Künste und Wissenschaften zwischen Aufklärung und Romantik: Netzwerke und Kulturen des Wissens*, eds. Cord-Friedrich Berghahn and Till Kinzel (Heidelberg: Universitätsverlag, Winter, 2013). A similar volume on Ebert, another of Lessing's important friends at Braunschweig, edited by Cord-Friedrich Berghahn, Gerd Biegel, and Till Kinzel, will appear in 2016.
35. See the important study by Michael Multhammer, *Lessings 'Rettungen.' Geschichte und Genese eines Denkstils* (Berlin: Walter de Gruyter, 2013).
36. LNPAW, 297.

An Epilogue

Josep Monserrat-Molas

Despite the similarities that one may draw between Baruch Spinoza and Leo Strauss as Jews or in their experience of exile or because of their shared interest in the theologico-political problem or their fueling of sustained controversies, the controversy excited by Spinoza in his lifetime appears in no way to be of the same class as that which has been stirred up by the figure of Strauss. The controversy over Strauss, however, does belong to the same uneasy relationship between philosophy and society, and it finds in Strauss's interest in Spinoza an example of the need to think through such a relationship. Unsurprisingly Strauss's most contentious thesis on the nature of philosophical texts has one of its milestones in his study of Spinoza's *Tractatus Theologico-Politicus*. That Strauss said the theologico-political problem was always his theme only further underscores the relevance of the considerations that follow.

Strauss's writings on Spinoza have two high points: his 1930 book *Spinoza's Critique of Religion* and his 1948 essay "How to Study Spinoza's *Theologico-Political Treatise*."[1] The gap in time between the two works coincides with the period that extends from the end of Strauss's training to the introduction of his seminal contribution to hermeneutics. To appreciate the exceptional nature of Strauss's study of Spinoza, a field that is after all not one of those in which he has had his greatest influence, it is valuable to note the Strauss added a special preface to the English translation of his German book of 1930 when it was published in the United States in 1962. In his preface, Strauss revisits his years of training, which culminated in his article on Carl Schmitt's concept of the political, included with the translation as an appendix.

One has at least two possible ways to approach Strauss's Spinoza: the first would sidestep his later hermeneutical theses on reticent writing, and it would give us a description of his *démarche*, while the second would take these theses on board and lead us to the core of his art of writing. In his 1962 preface, Strauss conceded that he read Spinoza differently after thirty years; but even so, he stood by his original text.[2] Spinoza was doubtless instrumental in Strauss's ability to move beyond his German context and served, too, as a weigh station toward his conception of the art of writing under persecution. The reissue of the 1930 text suggests that it still performed a function, at least to gain a proper understanding of the change of orientation in his investigations.

1. THE UNSUCCESSFUL SYNTHESIS

Leo Strauss strove to orient his scholarly vocation within the cultural and academic environment of Germany in the1920s. Born on the eve of the twentieth century, he was not distracted from pursuing a life of scholarship (perhaps as an eminent professor), on account of his family's status as Jewish, his service as a soldier in the German Empire in World War I, or because of a youthful summer flirtation with Zionism.[3] He studied at the University of Hamburg, one of the bastions of neo-Kantianism, and came under the tutelage particularly of Ernst Cassirer, whose then-current concern was the "problem of knowledge" and who was to act as Strauss's supervisor for his doctoral thesis, "On the Problem of Knowledge in the Philosophical Doctrine of F.H. Jacobi" (1921).[4] At the time, the reign of neo-Kantianism and phenomenology had turned the problem of knowledge into the central question of academic philosophy. Jacobi is well-known to have been inimical to Kantian criticism and German idealism, and he had been the man who instigated a debate with the Enlightenment Jew Moses Mendelssohn over the question of Lessing's Spinozism, or what later became known as the "the pantheism dispute." In 1929, Leo Strauss was named to the group of editors working on Mendelssohn's *Gesammelte Schriften*, which was being published to commemorate the bicentenary of Mendelssohn's birth. Strauss took charge of the second volume (published in 1931) and the first half of the third volume (1932). The second half of the third volume, however, did not appear in print until 1974, a year after Strauss's death.[5] This interruption is a clear sign of the violent effect of the twentieth century on the work of the Academy. The publication of the philosophical writings of Mendelssohn, an example of the assimilation of Judaism to German culture, cannot be separated from one of the driving themes of Strauss's inquiry—the relationship between philosophy and Judaism.[6]

One of the last pieces that Strauss published was an introduction to the English translation of Hermann Cohen's posthumous book in which he addresses the religion of reason and the sources of Judaism (1919).[7] Cohen, one of the founders of the Marburg school of neo-Kantian philosophy, viewed his Jewish writings as an appendix to a systematic philosophy of the methodical idealism of pure knowledge. He was a religious rationalist for whom revelation is the divine creation of reason and not a historical act: rational religion is not a historical religion, nor is purified Judaism according to his interpretation.[8] Judaism is not the absolute religion, yet it is also not simply another historical religion: Judaism, and only Judaism, is "pure monotheism." In Strauss's introduction, he points to the importance of the concept of 'source' for Cohen: the Jewish source is the origin of rational religion, something which no other religion can be; however, it needs Platonism and Kantianism to purify it in order to attain its proper expression.[9] For Strauss, both Moses Mendelssohn and Hermann Cohen represent the volatile (and indeed unsuccessful) synthesis of elements that have greater strength than the synthesis itself. From this perspective, it becomes clear why Strauss refers in "Jerusalem and Athens" (1967) to Cohen's lecture, "The Social Ideal in Plato and the Prophets,"[10] in which Plato and the prophets are posited as the two most important sources for the synthesis out of which modern culture has taken shape. Plato stands as the figure of scientific knowledge and rational ethics, while the prophets contribute something that is knowledge in only a metaphorical sense, but that is nevertheless indispensable: their belief that the conduct of a person can undergo a more drastic change than Plato was able to contemplate, precisely because the prophets lacked concepts of science and unchanging human nature. Thus Cohen gives us what Strauss explicitly calls the expression of the "Enlightenment ideal" voiced by "the greatest representative of German Jewry and spokesman for it."[11]

Though Strauss edited Mendelssohn and was a young admirer of Cohen, he eventually came to view the modern social idea of scientific rationalism animating Western culture in the years before World War I as a delusion and a deception. After World War I and the rise of the Soviet Union and Nazi Germany, what was obvious for Cohen, the superiority of the modern synthesis over its premodern components, was cast into doubt for Strauss. Eventually he would contend that the doubts hanging over moral progress have led to a crisis of civilization because the distinction between good and bad, or good and evil, has been replaced by the distinction between the progressive and the reactionary. Thus taking political philosophy as a gradual relativization of the concepts of good and bad, modern people are left without the conceptual tools needed to choose among values or alternative ways of living.[12]

For Cohen, who was partly modifying Kant, progress is not a question of faith, but a postulate of practical reason that had a status in the field of morality much like the status of mathematical postulates in the field of the natural sciences. Cohen conceives of progress as an essential part of rationalism, a part sufficient to give meaning to human dignity and happiness. Today such a belief in progress relies on the ingenuous goodness of a faith that confers on progressivism the certainty of a judgment requiring no rationale. In the name of classical rationalism, Strauss draws this lesson: the human being can seek to advance only by understanding and recognizing the necessity of his or her limits. The possibility of progress is rooted in an understanding of the unfinished and incomplete nature of human wisdom: "Because of the elusiveness of the whole, the beginning or the questions retain a greater evidence than the end or the answers; return to the beginning remains a constant necessity."[13] Because, as Strauss indicates in the book he published the year prior to his death, "We all are beginners."[14]

Strauss's return to classical political rationalism was a result of his elucidation of the clash between reason and revelation (Athens and Jerusalem), a conflict reopened for him with his analysis of the failure of progressivism. Strauss starts from the conviction that the Jewish world was clearly opposed to philosophy,[15]and he relates this issue or conflict to the devaluation of the first subject of philosophy—the heavens and the celestial bodies—in the opening chapter of *Genesis*, or the prohibition not to eat from the tree of the knowledge of good and evil in its second chapter, or the divine name "I Am that I Am," or the warning that the law is not in the heaven above or in the waters below, or the prophet Micah's words on what the Lord requires of people, or Talmudic pronouncements such as "he who reflects about four things—about what is above, what is below, what is before, what is behind—it would be better for him not to have come into the world." For Strauss, however, the status of philosophy in Judaism as well as in Islam was "not in every respect a misfortune."[16] The official recognition of philosophy in Christendom made it subject to ecclesiastical oversight.

By contrast, philosophy's precarious position in the Jewish and Islamic worlds also kept it strictly private, enabling it, paradoxically, to enjoy greater freedom. Strauss understood that in such a situation the status of philosophy resembled that which prevailed in the classical Greek world, an essentially private and transpolitical activity. Jewish and Islamic philosophers recognized the parallels between such a state of affairs and that of their own times. In the Greek city, the philosopher was in grave danger—a characterization ascribed by Alfarabi to Plato. Plato averted the danger through his art, but his success should not blind us to the existence of a danger which, however much its forms may vary, is in Strauss's words "always coeval with philosophy."[17]

Starting from the spiritual situation of German Judaism, and especially its state of dependence on the German cultural world at the time, Strauss focused on the relationship between "the rational" and "the irrational" in religious matters, underlining as he had done since his earliest writings the existence of a caesura, or break, between the conception of such a relationship in premodern theology and its modern counterpart:

> The earlier theology […] had the task of facilitating the victory of the "rational" moments of religion in their struggle against the primitive-irrational ones. Now that this task has been all too completely accomplished, the duty of theology in the present is the reverse. Starting from the real of the rational, it must advance by means of a conscientious and scientifically irreproachable presentation of the irrational to the construction of a system that is commensurate with its concern.

And Strauss underscores the contrast:

> While earlier theology speculated in a religiously closed vault, the new theology lives under the open sky, and must itself contribute, according to its ability, to the construction of the vault. Then, the primary fact was God; now, it is world, man, religious experience.[18]

2. THE SPINOZA VARIATION

In spite of the thesis on Jacobi, which he wrote under Cassirer, and the academic influence of neo-Kantianism, Strauss did not remain an adherent of this school:

> When I was still almost a boy, Husserl explained to me who at that time was a doubting and dubious adherent of the Marburg school of neo-Kantianism, the characteristic of his own work in about these terms: "The Marburg school begins with the roof, while I begin with the foundation."[19]

In order to obtain his Habilitation, Strauss continued his studies in the seminars of Edmund Husserl and Martin Heidegger in Freiburg at the same time that he was studying the latest works of Hermann Cohen and cementing his friendship with Franz Rosenzweig. The intellectual question that gripped the German universities of the time was how to move beyond Kant. The issue had burst onto the scene with the publication of Heidegger's *Kant and the Problem of Metaphysics* and the debate held between Heidegger and Cassirer in Davos in 1929. By contrast, Strauss pursued his own line of inquiry, moving on from his studies of Jacobi to Spinoza. By 1925, he had already begun a collaboration with the *Akademie für die Wissenschaft des Judentums* in Berlin, where he coincided with Abraham Joshua Heschel, the Maimonides scholar. The school in Berlin was similar to the *Freies Jüdischen Lehrhaus* that Rosenzweig had founded in Frankfurt am Mein in 1920.[20] Philosophy was to be used as a tool and weapon in the internal controversies of the Jewish intellectual world, and Strauss's positioning gives some idea of the dispute within the German Jewish community in the twenties, which arose between Hermann Cohen and those who supported the lifting of Spinoza's expulsion.

In the preface that he wrote in August 1962 for the US edition of *Spinoza's Critique of Religion*, a text that has been read both as "spiritual testament" and as self-criticism, Strauss recalls the weakness of German liberal democracy in the twenties, the dissatisfaction of the Germans with the modern world, their romantic nostalgia for the Middle Ages, the legacy of Goethe and of Bismarck, the opposition between the East and the West and, above, all, the precarious situation of the German Jews.[21] According to Carlo Altini, the inspiration for the *Akademie für die Wissenschaft des Judentums* came not only out of the specific conditions of Weimar Germany, but also out of the specific political and cultural circumstances of Jewry in the modern world, a situation most powerfully expressed for the young Strauss in the questions posed by Zionism in relation to a central problem: the redefinition of Jewish identity in the modern world. The Zionist project, which was represented in Germany at the time by the ideas of Leon Pinsker (1821–1891), Theodor Herzl (1860–1904), and Max Nordau (1849–1923), absorbed Strauss's youthful passions only briefly and soon gave way to a more critical appraisal of the Zionist proposition. His estrangement can be seen clearly in his 1923 essays in which he holds that Zionism's solution to the Jewish problem, the creation of a Jewish state, is simply a mirror image of the solution proposed by various liberal movements, some Jewish and some not, that were in favor of emancipation.[22] Both liberalism and Zionism saw the Jewish question as purely human and political in nature, and they overlooked the most essential aspect of Jewish tradition: the faith. Between the Zionist project and the assimilationist project, however, there was a distinction. Assimilation sought to deny the existence of the Jewish question precisely in that aspect where Zionism asserted its persistence. Nonetheless, while the difference is important from a human standpoint, it does not appear to have been crucial either in theory or in practice.[23]

Strauss's inquiry is directed at clarifying the act of revelation. As Antonio Lastra has clearly shown, Strauss presents revelation as Jacobi does, as an act and therefore as something that corresponds not to philosophy, which is a rational and demonstrative procedure, but rather to perception and emotion. For Strauss, the facticity of revelation is to be the subject of political study until it attains the level of philosophy. By contrast, Jacobi had declared in a discussion with Lessing that "there is no other philosophy than Spinoza's philosophy," and he equated such a philosophy with atheism. Thus philosophy was held up as a denial of God, and the act of revelation was, for Judaism, not only the guarantee of the existence of reality, but also the revelation of a law and a set of rules of conduct.[24]

As noted earlier, the context in which Strauss found himself was signaled by a concerted effort to break the stranglehold that neo-Kantianism and its attendant idea of progress exerted in the German universities. At the same time, outside the universities, a controversy was brewing within Judaism itself in relation to Cohen and the possibility of German assimilation for modern Judaism. One stage in the dispute was a series of public exchanges that took place in 1916–1917 between Hermann Cohen and Martin Buber on the subject of Zionism and the State. Cohen had defended the moral identity between Zionism and Germaness, while Buber, without foreseeing the consequences, argued for the denationalization and emigration of the Jewish community to Palestine. Cohen tried to show the conflict between religion and the State using the works of Spinoza and locating the thrust of Spinoza's message in the establishment, "against the claims of the Church," of "the right of the State to enact laws with respect to religious faiths and their beliefs."[25] For Cohen, Judaism could expect neither love nor comprehension from Spinoza. Strauss's reply appeared in a paper written in 1924 ("Cohen's Analysis of Spinoza's Bible Science") in which he sought to demonstrate that the *Tractatus Theologico-Politicus* was part of "the prevailing spirit of the seventeenth century" and there was no need to "give particular weight to the Jewish context of Spinoza's life" because his *Tractatus Theologico-Politicus* was addressed broadly to Europe and not specifically to the Jewish community. Strauss thought that rationalism could still be valid if it was separated from German romanticism, which "Jewish romanticism has copied." Ultimately the defense of rationalism is a defense of the State as final arbiter or judge, an outcome that becomes inevitable when any theory of reason is elevated above historical conditions. Spinoza warned of the danger posed to nascent liberalism by the rise of irrationalism in the form of mystical sects inasmuch as the aim of faith "is nothing other than obedience and piety."[26] By counterbalancing contrary conceptions of the State and of religion (or the Church), Spinoza's *libertas philosophandi* becomes the only freedom that can give legitimacy to the new order of things.[27]

Strauss's inquiry does not lie in the "confessional" area, but remains always in the rational-philosophical realm. This period of his output concludes with a major essay published in 1932, which is dedicated to an analysis of Carl Schmitt's concept of "the political," an exploration that was to lead him to a study of Hobbes.[28] But even his book on Spinoza is not a 'Jewish' book, bearing witness instead to his deep roots within the cultural climate of Weimar Germany.

3. RESISTANCE AGAINST DESTRUCTION

Strauss originally turned his attention to Spinoza at roughly the same time that a debate arose among German Jews on the occasion of the 250th anniversary of Spinoza's death (1677) and the *Akademie für die Wissenschaft des Judentums* began to take an interest. The flashpoint of the controversy was a call to lift Spinoza's expulsion from the Jewish community and initiate his rehabilitation on behalf of Judaism. Those favoring removal of the *cherem* against Spinoza included supporters from the "Judaism of the Torah" or "spiritual Judaism," which was to reach its crowning moment in the "new thinking" of Franz Rosenzweig (1886–1929),[29] as well as those from the "Judaism of the nation" or "pragmatic and political Judaism," who tended to be Zionists. Strauss's depiction of the situation is drily sardonic:

> There were two reasons why contemporary Jews were inclined to celebrate Spinoza. The first is Spinoza's assumed merit about mankind and only secondarily about the Jews; the second is his assumed merit about the Jewish people and only secondarily about mankind.[30]

For Strauss, what the dispute revealed, at heart, was the precarious political position of the Jews in the enfeebled liberal democracy of Weimar Germany. Cohen took a stance in opposition to the rehabilitation of Spinoza. Not only did he refuse even to consider a plea to remove the expulsion, but he also found the 'canonization' of Spinoza absurd. Cohen could not fathom how the spiritual branch, which understood Jewish religiosity as "experience" and as such not limited to a given culture, should fail to recognize that Spinoza's attacks against the Mosaic Law in his *Tractatus Theologico-Politicus* extended to any form of religiosity and therefore to any form "of religious experience." (Thus it covered even that reading of the *Tractatus* that did not view it as critical of the spiritual religiosity of the New Testament.) In response to the "Judaism of the nation and the culture," Cohen characterized Spinoza as a traitor to his people, who in the *Tractatus Theologico-Politicus* speaks as a Christian would speak against a Jew, humbling a carnal and particular Judaism, which commands hatred of thy enemy, in the face of a spiritual and universal Christianity, with its commandment to love thy neighbor. Cohen was critical of calls to lift the expulsion whether coming from those in a liberally correct position, in harmony with Rosenzweig's new thinking as a philosophical system and therefore in harmony with German culture and "universal philosophy," or coming from those who took a Zionist perspective, seeking to appropriate a universal figure in order to reintroduce him into the fold of Jewish national culture.[31] Cohen maintained this contradictory two-pronged critique because he saw the most flagrant contradictions in a great number of examples in the *Tractatus Theologico-Politicus*. He asserted that "there is no honest man capable of understanding, let alone overcoming, the contradictions of the *Tractatus Theologico-Politicus*"; and he ultimately passed the Spinoza case over to a psychological explanation, which he put down to some resentment or loathing that scarcely followed a logical pattern.[32]

Critically situating himself within this debate, Strauss accepted the challenge and sought to do justice both to Spinoza and to the theologico-political problem: to do so, he tried to examine the *Tractatus Theologico-Politicus* by asking whether Spinoza had actually succeeded in his refutation of orthodoxy.[33] Strauss may have felt some influence as a result of the subject entrusted to him by the *Akademie*—namely, Spinoza's Bible science;[34] but that alone offers no grounds to view his contribution as in any sense spurious, given that his most valuable theme, the relationship between modern rationalism and the critique of religion, explicitly informs the entire book. As Carlo Altini points out, no textual argument offers points of support to verify the existence of a caesura, or break, in Strauss's early period as Scholem has suggested; confronting the Jewish texts of the 1920s and 1930s demonstrates that the opposite is true; that is, that there is a substantial unity of theme and perspective, at least from Strauss's break with Zionism until his complete formulation of a theory of hermeneutics at the end of the 1930s.[35] Of course, a number of passages written by the younger Strauss show a gradual appreciation of the direction of his own interpretations. One need think only of the original Platonic perspective from which he interprets the prophetology of Maimonides in *Philosophy and Law* (1935). With the exception of the review of Otto's essay on the idea of the holy, the bibliographical sources of Strauss's early essays are notably confined to the Jewish world. However, the cultural mien of his work on Spinoza is undeniably more sweeping, at least from 1930 onwards, in that it emphasizes an awareness of the magnitude of Hobbes in the formation of the philosophical and political paradigm of modernity.[36]

Strauss's book *Spinoza's Critique of Religion* is divided into two unequal parts. The first part carries the title "The Tradition of the Critique of Religion": after an introduction, the first chapter examines the beginning of this tradition since Epicureanism; the second chapter looks at Uriel da Costa; the third turns to Isaac La Peyrère, and the fourth and final chapter of part 1 addresses Thomas Hobbes. The book's second and longer part is called "Spinoza's Critique of Religion," which after an introduction has six chapters numbered five to ten: the fifth chapter is a critique of orthodoxy; the sixth is entitled "The Critique of Maimonides"; the seventh deals with a critique of Calvin; the eighth is concerned with an analysis of revealed religion; the ninth looks at the State and the social function of religion, and the tenth and final chapter concludes with Spinoza's conception of the Bible and Bible science.

Strauss's main proposition holds that "the possibility of the critique of revealed religion depends on the possibility of the *system*"; that is, of philosophy itself, and it lies not in attempting to force nature to obey people, but in people obeying nature. God, wrote Spinoza, "directs nature according to the requirements of universal laws, not according to the requirements of the particular laws of human nature."[37] The critique of religion is a critique of the excessive expectations aroused by religion and the incomprehensible attributes of the *deus absconditus.* As Antonio Lastra has demonstrated, elucidating the social function reserved to religion calls for a deeper understanding of "the complex relation between political theory and political *ethos*."[38] The State, and not the community separated from social life, is the safeguard of security and morality in sufficient degree for the exercise of the intelligence. The difference in relation to Hobbes is that the State must be based on the freedom of its members: the ultimate reason of the State is not security or peace, but rather the conviction that inspires the citizens of a free state, as Spinoza writes in the final chapter of *Tractatus Theologico-Politicus.* Democracy or government by the many is possible only if human passions can be regulated by reason.

Strauss pursued a program that appears to be a path of moderation and restraint amid the "self-destruction of reason" produced by modernity:

> The victory of orthodoxy through the self-destruction of rational philosophy was not an unmitigated blessing, for it was a victory not of Jewish orthodoxy but of any orthodoxy, and Jewish orthodoxy based its claim to superiority to other religions from the beginning on its superior rationality (Deut. 4:6). Apart from this, the hierarchy of moralities and wills to which the final atheism referred could not but be claimed to be intrinsically true, theoretically true: 'the will to power' of the strong or of the weak may be the ground of every other doctrine; it is not the ground of the will to power: the will to power was said to be a fact.[39]

For Strauss, the true thinker must remain open to the possibility of living in a period that is inferior to the past: "One must be swayed by a sincere longing for the past."[40] To judge the past from the standpoint of the present is to presume that the present offers a better vantage than the past. The overcoming of this prejudice, which Strauss dates back to the close of his investigations in Germany, is bound up with his reflections on a forgotten way of writing from which he had borrowed a number of features in order to present results in a way that evinces a parallel way of reading. For instance, as Kenneth Hart Green has shrewdly noted, Strauss revised parts of the original German edition of his Spinoza book for the English translation, with the result that his demonstration of Spinoza's failure to refute revelation—that is, the chapter on Maimonides, became the central section of the book, the most important according to the esoteric hermeneutic rules that Strauss discovered in reticent writing.[41]

Because of their density, the writings of Leo Strauss can be entered from a variety of approaches. The first route would start by taking an interest in the authors to whom Strauss devoted his attention. For years, the engagement in polemics over Leo Strauss was, in fact, an engagement in polemics over many others such as Plato or Maimonides, Machiavelli or Hobbes, Spinoza or any philosopher who might be germane to a dispute. Gradually the focus on confrontations with other philosophers waned and interest shifted toward Strauss as the author of studies until eventually, and not for strictly academic reasons, it came to center primarily on his persona. The issue of how to gain access to Strauss is underpinned by the conviction that any effort to understand him must take the form of a greater dedication to the authors who engaged his attention. To the extent that Strauss was convinced both of the perennial natural of the fundamental problems that beset human life and of the fact that the philosophers have been crucially attentive to these problems, any entry point into Strauss may be a promising one, provided that our genuine concern is with human life and its problems. Indeed, since no exposition of the fundamental problems of human life can fully exhaust the magnitude of their complexity, no approach to Strauss will be more than an approximation.

NOTES

1. *RKS* and *SCR*. See Leo Strauss, "How to Study Spinoza's *Theologico-Political Treatise*," in *Proceedings of the American Academy for Jewish Research* 17 (1948): 69–131 (reprinted in *PAW*). Cf. Errol E. Harris, "Is There an Esoteric Doctrine in the *Tractatus Theologico-Politicus*?" in *Mededelingen vanwege het Spinozahuis* 38 (1978):1–19; Jacqueline Lagree, "Leo Strauss, lecteur de Spinoza: auteur ou lecteur, qui est le dieu caché?" in *Cahiers de philosophie politique et juridique de l'Université de Caen* 23 (1993):113–135; J. Montaux, "Exotérisme et philosophie: Leo Strauss et l'interprétation du *Traité théologico-politique*," in *Spinoza au XXe siècle. Actes des Journées d'études 1990 à la Sorbonne*, ed. Olivier Bloch (Paris: Presses Universitaires de France, 1993), 421–443; W. Soffer, "Modern Rationalism, Miracles and Revelation: Strauss' Critique of Spinoza," in *Leo Strauss: Political Philosopher and Jewish Thinker*, ed. K.L. Deutsch and W. Nicgorski (Lanham, MD: Rowman & Littlefield, 1994), 143–173; Omero Proietti, "*Teshuvah* per via obliqua. L'*antispinozismo* de Leo Strauss," in *Studia Spinoziana* 11 (1995): 81–110; Laurent Jaffro, "Spinoza: la question théologico-politique et la rhétorique de la philosophie," in *Figures du théologico-politique*, eds. E. Cattin, L. Jaffro, A. Petit (Paris: Vrin, 1999), 91–115; G. Bensussan, "Leo

Strauss et la modernité juive: Presence et retour," in *Leo Strauss: Art d'Écrire, politique, philosophie. Texte de 1941,* eds. L. Jaffro et al. (Paris: Vrin, 2001), 59–80; Heinrich Meier, *Leo Strauss and the theologico-political problem* (Cambridge: Cambridge University Press, 2006); Steven Smith, *Reading Leo Strauss. Politics, Philosophy, Judaism* (Chicago: University of Chicago Press, 2006); Matthew Sharpe, "Che Vuoi? Politico-Philosophical Remarks on Leo Strauss' *Spinoza*," in *The Bible and Critical Theory* 3/3 (2007): 41.1–14.

2. "The present study was based on the premise, sanctioned by powerful prejudice, that a return to pre-modern philosophy is impossible. The change of orientation which found its first expression, not entirely by accident, in the article published at the end of this volume [on Carl Schmitt] compelled me to engage in a number of studies in the course of which I became ever more attentive to the manner in which heterodox thinkers of earlier ages wrote their books. As a consequence of this, I now read the *Theologico-Political Treatise* differently than I read it when I was young. I understood Spinoza too literally because I did not read him literally enough." (Preface, *SCR*, 31)
3. "I was brought up in a conservative, even orthodox Jewish home somewhere in a rural district of Germany. The 'ceremonial' laws were rather strictly observed but there was very little Jewish knowledge. In the Gymnasium I became exposed to the message of German humanism. Furtively I read Schopenhauer and Nietzsche. When I was 16 and we read the Laches in school, I formed the plan, or the wish, to spend my life reading Plato and breeding rabbits while earning my livelihood as a rural postmaster. Without being aware of it, I had moved rather far away from my Jewish home, without any rebellion. When I was 17, I was converted to Zionism—to simple, straightforward political Zionism." (Leo Strauss, "A Giving of Accounts," in *JPCM*, 459–460). Cf. Steven Smith, "Leo Strauss. The Outlines of a Life," in *The Cambridge Companion to Leo Strauss,* ed. Steven Smith (Cambridge: Cambridge University Press, 2009), 13–40.
4. Leo Strauss, "Das Erkentnissproblem in der philosophischen Lehre F. H. Jacobis," (Hamburg, 1921), in *GS 2*. Carlo Altini (*Leo Strauss.*

Linguaggio del potere e linguaggio della filosofía [Bologna: Il Mulino, 2000], 54n.) cautions that the tone of this first study of Strauss is purely academic, confined to a thematic reconstruction of Jacobi's theory of knowledge, and does not tackle any of the theologico-political problems that become hallmarks of later works by Strauss. However, one can find a particular attention being given to the subjects of belief and skepticism (as distinct from relativism), filtered through a strong engagement with the classics (from Descartes to Kant and from Spinoza to Hume) in an effort to define some of the features of modern rationalism and subjectivism in the origins of the concept of value.

5. Moses Mendelssohn, *Gesammelte Schriften: Jubiläumsausgabe* (Berlin: Akademie-Verlag, 1931–1932); (Stuttgart-Bad Canstatt: Friedrich Fromman, 1974). Strauss's introductions can also be found in English in *LSMM*.
6. His first writings on these issues appeared in the 1920s in the journals *Juedische Rundschau* and *Der Jude*, a publication founded by Martin Buber, who was a friend of Franz Rosenzweig. See *GS 2*, EW, *JPCM*, and *LSMC*.
7. Leo Strauss, "Introductory Essay," in Hermann Cohen, *Religion of Reason Out of the Sources of Judaism* (New York: Frederick Ungar, 1972), xxiii–xxviii (reprint in *SPPP*).
8. Hermann Cohen, *Jüdische Schriften* (Berlin: Schwetschke, 1924).
9. Leo Strauss, "Introductory Essay," in *SPPP*, 234.
10. Cohen, *Jüdische Schriften* vol. I, 306–330. Cf. Leo Strauss, "Jerusalem and Athens. Some Preliminary Reflections" (1967), in *SPPP*, 147–173.
11. *SPPP*, 24.
12. PR. Cf. "Introduction," in *OT*.
13. *CM*, 21.
14. *XS*, 3.
15. Leo Strauss noted that even as late as 1765, Mendelssohn still considered it necessary to defend the study of logic and demonstrate that the prohibition against the reading of profane books did not pertain to works of logic. Cf. Moses Mendelssohn, *Gesammelte Schriften. Jubiläums Ausgabe*, vol. 2, 202–207; *PAW*, 20.

16. *PAW*, 21.
17. *PAW*, 21.
18. Leo Strauss, "Das Heilige," in *Der Jude* 7/4 (1923): 240–242 ("The Holy [1923])," in *EW*, 76–77.
19. Leo Strauss, "Philosophy as Rigorous Science and Political Philosophy," in *SPPP*, 31.
20. The *Akademie für die Wissenschaft des Judentums* was founded in Berlin in 1919 on the basis of a program devised by Franz Rosenzweig. Cf. a 1927 letter to Hermann Cohen: "Zeit ist's," in Franz Rosenzweig, *Zweistromland. Kleinere Schriften zu Glauben und Denken* (Dordrecht: Martinus Nijhoff, 1984), 461–481. The Academy was above all a research institute that provided grants to young researchers to undertake Hebrew studies in a variety of fields, ranging from philosophy to the Talmud, and from the Kabbalah to literature.
21. Leo Strauss, "Preface," in *SCR*, 3–4.
22. For example, "Der Zionismus bei Nordau," in *Der Jude* (1923), "Cohen's Analyse der Bibelwissenschaft Spinozas," in *Der Jude* (1924); "Zur Auseinandersetzung mit der europäischen Wissenschaft," in *Der Jude* (1924); "Biblische Geschichte und Wissenschaft," in *Juedische Rundschau* (1925) [English translation in *EW*].
23. See Carlo Altini, *Leo Strauss. Linguaggio del potere,* (Bologna: Il Mulino), 33–35.
24. Antonio Lastra, *La naturaleza de la filosofía política. Un ensayo sobre Leo Strauss* (Murcia: Res Publica, 2000), 66–67.
25. Hermann Cohen, "Spinoza über Staat und Religion, Judentum und Christentum," in *Jahrbuch für Geschichte und Literatur* 18 (1915): 56–151. Cf. Irene Abigail Piccinini, *Una guida fedele. L'influenza di Hermann Cohen sul pensiero di Leo Strauss* (Turin: Trauben, 2007).
26. Spinoza, *Tractatus Theologico-Politicus*, ch.14, 179.
27. Leo Strauss, "Cohens Analyse der Bibel-Wissenschaft Spinozas," in *Der Jude* 8 (1924): 295–314. In addition to Strauss's text, my argumentation draws on Lastra, *La naturaleza de la filosofía política*, 69–70. An additional piece by Strauss written prior to his Spinoza book ("Zur Bibelwissenschaft Spinozas und seiner Vorläufer," in *Korrespondenzblatt des Vereins zur Gründung und Erhaltung einer*

Akademie für die Wissenschaft des Judentums 7 [1926]:1–22) offers a framework for his 1930 work, though he had not yet completed his studies on Epicureanism and on Hobbes.

28. Leo Strauss, "Anmerkungen zu Carl Schmitt, *Der Begriff des Politischen,*" in *Archiv für Sozialwissenschaft und Sozialpolitik* 67 (1932): 732–749. Cf. Heinrich Meier, *Carl Schmitt and Leo Strauss. The Hidden Dialogue*, rev. ed., trans. J. Harvey Lomax with a "Preface to the American Edition" and a "Foreword" by Joseph Cropsey (Chicago: University of Chicago Press, 2006).
29. Franz Rosenzweig, *Star of Redemption*, trans. Barbara E. Galli (Madison, WI: University of Wisconsin Press, 2005) (*Stern der Erlösung*, 1921). Cf. Irene A. Piccinini, "Hermann Cohen et Franz Rosenzweig: deux modèles d'identité juive dans la pensée de Leo Strauss," in *Héritages de Franz Rosenzweig*, ed. M. Bienenstock (Paris: Editions de l'Éclat, 2011), 149–164.
30. Leo Strauss, "Preface," *SCR*, 15.
31. "[Spinoza] became the sole father of that new Church which was to be universal in fact and not merely in claim, like other Churches, because its foundation was no longer any positive revelation. It was a Church whose rulers were not priests or pastors but philosophers and artists and whose flock were the circles of culture and prosperity. [. . .] The new Church would transform Jews and Christians into human beings—into human beings of a certain kind: cultured human beings, human beings who because they possessed Science and Art did not need religion in addition. The new society, constituted by the aspiration common to all its members toward the True, the Good, and the Beautiful, emancipated the Jews in Germany. [. . .] In a word, the non-Jewish world, having been molded to a considerable extent by Spinoza, had become receptive to Jews who were willing to assimilate themselves to it." (Strauss, "Preface," *SCR,* 17)
32. Hermann Cohen, "Spinoza über Staat und Religion, Judentum und Chistentum," 290–372.
33. Leo Strauss, "Preface," *SCR*, 26.
34. For more information on the commission from Julius Guttmann, who was head of the school at the time; Cf. *RKS* in *GS 1*, ix.

35. Cf. Carlo Altini, *Leo Strauss. Linguaggio del potere*, 55–57, refuting the opinion of Heinrich Meier, editor of Strauss's *GS 1*, ix–xiv, who uses news from Strauss's letters to Gerhard Krüger and Gershom Scholem. Rémi Brague, "Leo Strauss et les medievaux" (in *Leo Strauss: Art d'écrire, politique, philosophie. Texte de 1941*, 121–130) provides new input on the exchanges between Meier and Altini over the Strauss's earliest thinking about the art of writing "between the lines."
36. Cf. Josep Monserrat-Molas, "Leo Strauss, *The Political Philosophy of Hobbes: Its Basis and Its Genesis* (1936)," in *Anuari de la Societat Catalana de Filosofia* 12 (2000): 25–39.
37. Spinoza, *Tractatus Theologico-Politicus*, ch. 6, 88.
38. Antonio Lastra, *La naturaleza de la filosofía política*, 64–80, especially page 79, from which many of the above observations are taken.
39. Leo Strauss, "Preface," in *SCR*, 30. Strauss published "The Legacy of Spinoza" in 1932 on the tricentenary of Spinoza's birth: Spinoza will endure because of his independence (*Unabhängigkeit*). Leo Strauss, "Das Testament Spinozas," in *Bayerische Israelitische Gemeindezeitung* 8/21 (1932): 322–326 (in *GS 1*, 415–422; *EW*, 216–223).
40. OCPH, 585. Cf. the beginning of *CM*, 1.
41. Kenneth Hart Green, *Jew and Philosopher. The Return to Maimonides in the Jewish Thought of Leo Strauss* (Albany: State University of New York Press, 1993), 152n17. The problem of reticence in philosophical literature, seen as a hallmark of the difference between political life and philosophical life, was to take shape in 1939, most notably in the essays on Xenophon and Lessing (SSTX; ET).

NOTES ON CONTRIBUTORS

Antonio Lastra, PhD, is the external researcher for the Instituto Franklin de Investigación en Estudios Norteamericanos at the Universidad de Alcalá (Spain). He is the editor in chief of *La Torre del Virrey: Revista de Estudios Culturales* and author of *La naturaleza de la filosofía política. Un ensayo sobre Leo Strauss* (2000), *Emerson como educador* (2007), *Ecología de la cultura* (2008), *Constitución y arte de escribir* (2009), *La filosofía y los dioses de la ciudad* (2011), and *La necesidad logográfica* (2014). He has translated Leo Strauss's *Persecución y arte de escribir y otros ensayos de filosofía política* (1996); Strauss and Eric Voegelin's *Fe y filosofía* (2009), coedited by Bernat Torres; Strauss and Gershom Scholem's *Correspondencia* (2009), coedited by Javier Alcoriza, and Strauss's *El libro de Maimónides* (2012) and *Sin ciudades no hay filósofos* (2014), both coedited by Raúl Miranda.

Carlo Altini is scientific director of the Fondazione San Carlo (Modena) and professor of history of philosophy at Modena and Reggio Emilia University. He has organized international symposiums in collaboration with École pratique des hautes études (Paris), Universität Erfurt and Scuola Normale Superiore (Pisa). As a member of the editorial board of the journal *Filosofia politica*, he was speaker at conferences and seminars in many universities (Paris, Jerusalem, Florence, Rome,

Uppsala, Cordoba, Pisa, Padua, Turin, Milan, Venice, Tilburg, Lausanne). He has published many books and essays in journals (*Rivista di filosofia, Giornale critico della filosofia italiana, Iride, Intersezioni, La società degli individui, La cultura, MicroMega, Il Ponte, History of European Ideas, Hobbes Studies, Interpretation: A Journal of Bible and Theology, Philosophy & Social Criticism, Comprendre,* and *Res Publica*) on Machiavelli, Hobbes, Spinoza, Carl Schmitt, Leo Strauss, Alexandre Kojève, Gershom Scholem, Karl Löwith, and Robin G. Collingwood.

Alessandra Fussi is associate professor of moral philosophy at the University of Pisa. She is the author of *Retorica e potere: Una lettura del Gorgia di Platone* (Pisa, 2006), and *La città nell'anima: Leo Strauss lettore di Platone e Senofonte* (Pisa, 2012). She has written numerous essays in several languages and published in international journals especially on the works of Plato, Aristotle, Leo Strauss, and Bernard Williams. Her most recent work focuses on the nature and role of the emotions of self-assessment in the ethical life. She has been a visiting professor at the Department of Philosophy at Boston University.

Jordi R. Sales-Coderch, PhD, is professor emeritus at the Faculty of Philosophy at the University of Barcelona. He has been dean of this Faculty (1995–1998, 2006–2009) and president of the Catalan Society of Philosophy (1989–2001). He has published *Coneixement i situació* (Barcelona, 1990; 2nd ed., 2014); *Introducció a la lectura de Leo Strauss* (Barcelona, 1991), with Josep Monserrat-Molas; *Estudis sobre l'ensenyament platònic,* vol. 1: *Figures i Desplaçaments* (Barcelona, 1992), and vol. 2: *A la flama del vi. El Convit platònic, filosofia de la transmissió* (Barcelona, 1996); and *La captivitat inadvertida* (Barcelona, 2013). Sales-Coderch is co-editor of the *Anuari de la Societat Catalana de Filosofia* and has published numerous articles on Platonic philosophy, seventeenth-century philosophy, and on Kant and phenomenology.

Mauro Farnesi Camellone is senior research fellow at the Department of Political Studies, Law and International Relationships, University of Padua, and member of the International Centre for a European

Legal and Political Lexicon. He is member of the board of the international review *Filosofia Politica*. He is author of the books *Giustizia e storia. Saggio su Leo Strauss* (2007); *La politica e l'immagine. Saggio su Ernst Bloch* (2009); *Indocili soggetti. La politica teologica di Thomas Hobbes* (2013).

TILL KINZEL received his PhD (2002) and Habilitation (2005) from the Technical University of Berlin. He has published books on Allan Bloom (*Platonische Kulturkritik in Amerika*, 2002), Nicolás Gómez Dávila (*Nicolás Gómez Dávila*, 2003; 4th enlarged ed., 2015), Philip Roth (*Die Tragödie und Komödie des amerikanischen Lebens*, 2006), and Michael Oakeshott (2007). Most recently he has edited writings by Johann Joachim Eschenburg (*Von Chaucer zu Pope*; *Über William Hogarth und seine Erklärer* [both in 2013]; *Kleine Geschichte des Romans von der Antike bis zur Aufklärung*, 2014), and Edward Gibbon. With Jarmila Mildorf he co-edited *Imaginary Dialogues in English* (2012) and *Imaginary Dialogues in American Literature and Philosophy* (2014). With Cord-Friedrich Berghahn he co-edited *Johann Joachim Eschenburg und die Künste und Wissenschaften zwischen Aufklärung und Romantik* (2013) and a book on the reception of Edward Gibbon in Germany (2015).

JOSEP MONSERRAT-MOLAS, PhD, is professor of philosophy at the University of Barcelona, research director of *Eidos. Platonism and Modernity*, and co-editor of *Anuari de la Societat Catalana de Filosofia*. He is the author of *El Polític de Plató. La gràcia de la mesura* (Barcelona, 1999); *Estranys, setciències i pentatletes. Cinc estudis de filosofia política clàssica* (Barcelona, 2007); and *Al margen del Político de Platón* (Barcelona, 2012). Monserrat-Molas has also edited *Hermenèutica i platonisme* (Barcelona, 2002), *Idees d'Autoritat* (Barcelona, 2002), *Pensament i Filosofia a Catalunya* (3 vols., Barcelona, 2002–2004, with Pompeu Casanovas), *Herencias Straussianas* (Valencia, 2004, with Antonio Lastra), *Philosophy and Dialog* (2 vols.) (Barcelona, 2007 and 2010, with Antoni Bosch-Veciana), *Hermenèutica & Modernitat*, (Barcelona, 2009, with Jordi Sales-Coderch), *Formal Structures in Plato's Dialogues*, (Sankt

Agustin, 2011, with Francisco Lisi and Maurizio Migliori), and *Aristòtil lector del Fileb. Lectures sobre el Fileb Platònic* (Barcelona, 2012, with Bernat Torres). He has translated into Catalan Strauss's articles, *The City and Man* and "The Problem of Socrates."

INDEX

Alcibiades, 41, 77
Alfarabi (Fārābī), xiv, xv, xxin13, 84, 98n15, n16, 121
Altini, Carlo, 15, 123, 127, 132n4, 133n23, 135n35, 137
Altmann, Alexander, 9, 14n17, 103
Anastaplo, George, xxin11, 67
Antiphanes of Chio, 15, 17
Anscombe, Elisabeth, 70
Arendt, Hannah, x, 63, 70
Aristophanes, 4, 18, 43, 49, 68
Aristotle, xvi, 17, 24, 43, 63nn5–6, 68, 70–75, 79n16, 100n44, 101, 138
Aubenque, Pierre, 73, 78n7
Averroes, xxn6, 34
Avicenna, 34

Bacon, Francis, 105
Benardete, Seth, 66n22, 67, 68, 78n1
Bloom, Allan, xxn8, 10n1, 12n6, 64n14, 139
Buber, Martin, 124, 132n6

Calvin, Jean, 128
Cassirer, Ernst, x, xixn4, xxn5, 105, 118, 122, 123
Cervantes, Miguel de, 101, 111n1, 114
Cicero, 74, 105
Cohen, Hermann, xvii, xxiin18
Collingwood, Robin George, 16, 17, 21, 27, 28, 29, 42n3, 52, 58, 64n9, 138
Cordell, Joan Crystal, 71, 78n8
Costa, Uriel da, 128
Croce, Benedetto, 16
Cropsey, Josep, 11n5, 134n28

Dewey, John, 16
Descartes, René, 17, 21, 105, 106, 132n4
Diderot, Denis, 4
Dilthey, Wilhelm, 16

Finnis, John, 70
Fichte, Johann Gottlieb, 50
Fittbogen, Gottfried, 104

Gadamer, Hans-Georg, x, 12n7, 16, 50, 64n8, 68, 71
Garin, Eugenio, 16
Gentile, Giovanni, 16

Goethe, Johann Wolfgang von, 4, 9, 14n17, 123
Goeze, Johan Melchior, 108, 109
Goldschmidt, Victor, 72, 78n9
Green, Kenneth Hart, xvii, 21n14, 13n14, 111n4, 129, 135n41
Gramsci, Antonio, 16

Ha-Levi, Jehuda, 10
Heidegger, Martin, ix, x, xvii, xixnn2–3, xxn6, xxin14, xiin18, 5, 16, 20, 21, 50, 63n2, 122, 123
Hegel, Georg Wilhelm Friedrich, 15–17, 21, 31, 35, 72
Herodotus, 43, 63n1
Heschel, Abraham Joshua, 123
Herzl, Theodor, 123
Hobbes, Thomas, xxn6, 5, 17, 18, 33, 34, 44, 101, 125, 127–129, 134n27, 138
Homer, 77
Hume, David, 21, 132n4

Jacobi, Friedrich Heinrich, x, xxn5, 6–9, 104, 105, 113n15, 19, 118, 122–124, 132n4

Kant, Immanuel, x, xixn4, 21, 24, 31, 44, 50, 102, 118–120, 123, 132n4, 138
Klein, Jacob, x, xxin14, 8, 10n1, 13n14, 68, 111n1
Kojève, Alexandre, 68, 138
Krüger, Gerhard, x, 68, 111n2, 135n35

La Mothe Le Vayer, François de, 71
Lampert, Laurence, 10n1, 11n5, 12n7, 103, 112n12
La Peyrère, Isaac, 128
Lastra, Antonio, xviii, 1, 124, 128, 133n24, 134n27, 135n38
Leibniz, Gottfried, 44, 106, 112n7
LeQuire, Alan, 76
Lessing, Gotthold Ephraim, xv, 4–9, 12n11, 13nn13–14, 14n17, 101–115, 119, 124, 136
Lippmann, Walter, 69
Locke, John, 18
Löwith, Karl, x, 12n11, 68, 101, 107, 111n3, 138
Lucretius, 43, 77, 105

MacIntyre, Alasdair, 70
Machiavelli, Niccolò, 4, 13n14, 18, 33, 34, 79n16, 101, 105, 129, 138
Mendelssohn, Moses, 5–9, 13n13, 14n17, 102–105, 109, 112n5–7, 119, 120, 132n5, 133n15
Monserrat-Molas, Josep, 67, 79n27, 117–136, 138

Nietzsche, Friedrich, xii, xiii, xv, xvi, 1–5, 7, 10n1, 11nn4–5, 12nn7–9, 13n14, 14n17, 18, 21, 51, 105, 114n26, 131n3
Nordau, Max, 123

Otto, Rudolf, 127

Pangle, Thomas L., xxn8, 10n1, 42n3, 111nn1–4, 112n11
Pellegrin, Pierre, 73
Pericles, 77
Petronius, 4
Pinsker, Leon, 123
Plato, x, xii–xvi, xixn4, 1, 3, 4, 7–9, 10nn1–3, 11n4, 12n5–7, 14n17, 15, 17, 18, 21, 27, 30, 32–34, 41, 43–53, 56, 58, 61, 62, 63n5–7, 64n14, 66n25, 68, 74, 77, 81, 82, 84–87, 91, 92, 94, 96–100, 101, 104–106, 114n25, 119, 120, 121, 127, 129, 131n3, 138

Plutarch, 15, 17, 42n1
Polemarchus, 55, 56, 59

Raz, Joseph, 70
Reimarus, Herman Samuel, 109
Richelieu (Cardinal), 71
Romilly, Jacqueline de, 77, 79n25
Rorty, Richard, 67
Rosen, Stanley, xxn6, 66n25, 67
Rosenzweig, Franz, 123, 126, 132, 133n20, 134n29
Rousseau, Jean-Jacques, 18, 105, 106

Schleiermacher, Friedrich, xxin10
Schmitt, Carl, 5, 21, 112 n. 5, 118, 125, 131n2, 138
Scholem, Gershom, xxn6, 11n3, 68, 127, 135n35, 137, 138
Socrates, x, xii, xixn3, 4, 8, 9, 10n3, 12n6, 13n16, 41, 45, 47–50, 54–57, 59–62, 64n17, 66n22, 75, 77, 81–85, 87, 93, 95, 100n55, 101
Sontag, Susan, 67
Sorensen, A. D., 73
Sparshott, Francis, 73, 78n14, 79n17
Spengler, Oswald, 18, 68, 69
Spinoza, Baruch, 5–9, 13n13, 17, 18, 33, 34, 101, 104, 106, 117, 118, 122–129, 131n2, 132n4, 134nn27–31, 135nn37–39, 138
Steiner, George, 67
Sterne, Laurence, 114n26
Swift, Jonathan, 101, 102, 105, 107, 114n26

Tovar, Antonio, 73
Thucydides, 11n5, 18, 43, 68, 70, 75–77
Tricot, A., 73

Volpi, Franco, 71, 78n7
Voltaire, 4

Weber, Max, 21–25

Xenophon, 7, 10n1, 11n5, 18, 33, 34, 43, 45, 49, 75, 101, 105, 136

Yaffe, Martin D., xviii, 13nn12–13, 102